Robin Smith's
Batting Skills

Robin Smith's Batting Skills

A Complete Step-By-Step Guide

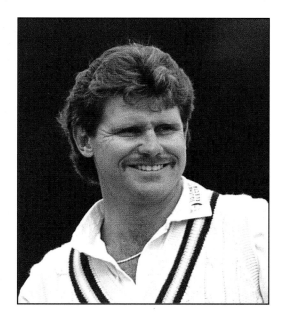

Specially commissioned photography by Action Plus

Dedication To my father, John Smith, who has given me all the encouragement and enthusiasm I could ever have wished for and the hours and hours of practice spent with me. To Grayson Heath who has been my coach from day one and who has helped me to develop my batting skills and technique.

Acknowledgements There are many people to thank for their help and co-operation in putting together this book. In particular I would like to thank Mike Taylor and Tony Baker at Hampshire CCC for allowing us to use the County Ground at Southampton for the photographic shoot, and the groundsman, Nigel Gray, for preparing the strip despite the soggy conditions that week. Many thanks to Adrian Aymes, Kevan James and Darren Flint for their help with bowling and fielding during the session. Thanks too to John Gray of Gray Nicholls who provided the equipment used. Lastly I must acknowledge the cheerful and skilled assistance of John Crace who helped me to put my ideas into words during the course of several enjoyable afternoons.

Picture Acknowledgements
Front jacket photograph by Patrick Eagar.
Allsport 8,/Chris Cole 58, /Adrian Murrell 9 top, 29 left, 48, 51 bottom/Ian Murrell 28 bottom left, 59/Ben Radford 1, 6, 9 bottom *Colorsport* 3, 4, 24 bottom right, 27, 62 right, 63 left and right
Patrick Eagar 35, 41 top, 49 right, 50 top, 60 right, 62 left

First published in Great Britain in 1994 by Hamlyn an imprint of Reed Consumer Books Limited, Michelin House, 81 Fulham Road, London SW3 6RB and Auckland, Melbourne, Singapore and Toronto

Project Editor: David Heslam, *Art Editor:* Bryan Dunn
Designed by: Vivien J McDonald – Vivitext Creative Services
Picture Research: Claire Taylor, *Production Controller:* Michelle Thomas

Printed and bound in Great Britain by
Butler & Tanner Ltd, Frome and London

Contents

Introduction

IF YOU are hoping that by reading this book you will instantly become a top class batsman, then I must disappoint you right at the start. No book can be a substitute for practice in the nets and playing in the middle.

However, a book can be a great help. There's no point endlessly practising if you are doing things in the wrong way, because that will only reinforce bad habits. Even if you do have a coach to help you, it is amazing how quickly you can forget what he says. A coach rarely explains in great detail what he is asking you to do because he can give a visual demonstration. He will say things like: 'Do it this way' or 'Hold the bat like this' as he shows you what to do. So it can be handy to have something concrete to which you can refer back time and again, until you have the ideas locked firmly in your mind.

I also hope that this book will in some way inspire you to want to play the game. When I was young I would spend hours trying to emulate my elder brother Chris, who was my first hero, and as I grew older so I began to draw inspiration from watching Test batsmen. My first coach, Grayson Heath, always contended that the power of imitation should never be underestimated. He believed that, even without any formal coaching, a boy who wanted to succeed badly enough could do so just by watching the great players and practising hard. If the words and pictures of this book inspire you to practise or go to a game, then it will have done its job.

How hard should you practise? This is hard

for me to say, because my father would get me up at 4.30 every morning to practise a variety of sports. In the beginning there were days when I felt like a lie in, and my Mum was often telling my Dad that he was pushing me too hard. However, it wasn't long before I began to get some good results, representing my school at both cricket and rugby, and breaking 26 school athletics records. With this success, it got to the point where I was bullying Dad to get up early!

I do believe that I was born with a God-given talent for cricket, but my talent needed the practice to become fully realized. I'm not sure that you need to practise quite as hard as I did, though. Apart from anything else, this country is just too cold for most of the year to make getting up that early anything other than a deeply unpleasant experience!

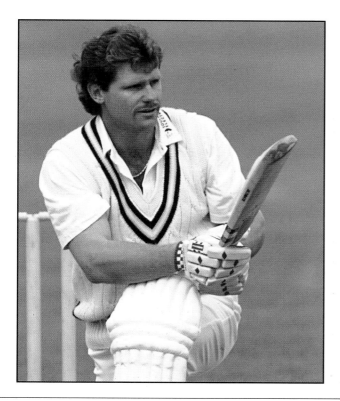

The purpose of this book is not to make you into a first-class cricketer. Yet don't be without ambition. First-class cricketers aren't a different species to ordinary cricketers. Grayson Heath always used to say that if he was given a 10-year-old boy he could guarantee that he played first-class cricket. There were just two requirements. The first was that he should have ball-sense, which applies to about 70% of the population. The second was that he should want to play enough to put the necessary practice in. So if you think both categories apply to you, then don't be afraid to go for it.

Above all, though, I would like you to enjoy the game. I've always found that the more effort I put into something, the more I enjoy it, but that does not mean that you should take things to excess. Try to become the best cricketer that you can possibly be, and be happy with the level you reach. It may be that the time you spend at school or at work does not give you enough spare time to practise and do all the other things you want to do.

If this is the case, then so be it. Don't push yourself so hard that cricket becomes a chore. A friendly game of village cricket can be just as hard fought and enjoyable as a three-day county game. Indeed, I would say that more often than not the village game was more fun!

So enjoy the book, and enjoy your cricket.

Robin Smith Factfile

ROBIN Smith was born in Durban, South Africa, on 13 September 1963. He is the younger brother of Chris Smith, who also played for Hampshire and England.

At school in South Africa he broke 26 athletics records and also broke the point and run scoring records for the rugby and cricket teams. He later became the South African U-17 shot putt champion, and represented the South African Schools at cricket in 1979-80.

Robin joined Hampshire CCC in 1981. Prompted by his elder brother, the county had invited Robin to England for a three week trial, and then given him a contract after just three days. His first-class opportunities were limited to start with as he was just one of four overseas players, and the regulations only permitted the county to field two in any one game.

Robin had made his first-class debut for Natal in January 1981, but it was not until the following year that he made his English first-class debut for Hampshire v Pakistan. He played his first county championship match in 1983 when he scored an unbeaten 100 against Lancashire. He qualified as an English player in 1985 and has been the linchpin of the Hampshire batting ever since.

He was first picked to play for England in the fourth Test of the 1988 series against the West Indies at Headingley. Although England lost the game, Robin impressed everyone with his courage and aggression while facing the West Indian quartet of fast bowlers. His 100 partnership with Allan Lamb in the first innings was the high spot of the match as far as England was concerned.

That game was the beginning of a remarkable run, broken only by injury, in the England Test side of 45 games. This ended when Robin was omitted from the team for the 6th Test against Australia in 1993. During this period Robin scored 8 centuries and 22 half centuries and had the impressive average of 46.24.

Robin's first Test century came against the Australians in 1989 and his most recent against Sri Lanka in

Playing for Hampshire against Oxford University at The Parks, Robin executes the fearsome square cut that most cover points never get near.

Robin cover drives during his one-day century off New Zealand in 1990.

Robin Smith's Career Batting Statistics

First Class Cricket

BATTING:	Mat	Inns	No	Runs	HS	Avge	100s
for Hampshire	161	267	46	10205	209*	46.17	28
for other teams	48	80	12	2617	149*	38.48	3
for England	45	84	14	3237	148*	46.24	8
TOTALS	254	431	72	16059	209*	44.73	39

One-Day Internationals

BATTING:	Mat	Inns	No	Runs	HS	Avge	100s
for England	58	57	8	2068	167*	42.20	4

One-Day Cricket

BATTING:	Mat	Inns	No	Runs	HS	Avge	100s
for Hampshire	165	158	28	6380	155*	49.07	13

Colombo in 1993. In between he has scored centuries against all the other Test playing nations, other than South Africa and Zimbabwe whom he has never faced, and New Zealand, against whom his highest score remains 96.

Robin was named as one of Wisden's five cricketers of the year in 1989, and is widely recognized as one of the best players of fast bowling in the world today. His record against spin is not quite so impressive, but Robin is a top class batsman with fighting qualities, and few people doubt that he will soon be equally at home against spin as pace, and that he will continue to be the backbone of the England batting line-up for many years to come.

Pulling another boundary through mid-wicket during his 121 against India in the first innings of the 2nd Test at Old Trafford in 1990.

9

Choosing Your Equipment

IF your job when you go out to bat is to score runs for your team, then your bat, pads, gloves etc. are the tools of your trade. As with any job, the more physically and mentally comfortable you feel with your equipment, the better you will perform. The perfect bat or pad does not exist; what feels right for me would feel awkward for David Gower, and vice versa. Everyone has their own peculiarities and individual preferences, and what is important is to find something that feels comfortable for you.

Even as a complete beginner to the game you will instinctively feel that one bat feels better in your hands than another. Learn to trust that instinct. Having said that, there are some general guidelines you should follow when buying cricket equipment. At the very least they will help to save time in making your choice, they may save you money and, at best, they can help you to avoid getting into bad habits.

The Bat

Ideally you should be able to rest the bat between your legs, so that the top of the handle just touches your groin. If it does, then the bat is the right height for you. Of course, sometimes you may have to make do. A bat is an expensive piece of equipment, and while you are still growing you may have to use one that is too small unless you can afford to replace it each year.

Assuming that you have found a selection of bats of the right height, you then have to choose what weight of bat you prefer. Over the last ten to fifteen years there has been a tendency for professional cricketers to favour heavier and heavier bats. Ian Botham's bat was often compared to a railway sleeper! A heavy bat has its advantages - you can hit the ball extremely hard and even mis-hits can carry for six. Don't forget, though, that you need to be immensely strong to wield a bat of 3lb or so effectively. Just because your hero uses a heavy bat, does not make it right for you. Try to choose one that suits your style of play. My bat weighs 3lb with most of the weight in the toe end of the bat, because I like to punch at the ball. David Gower's bat weighed 2lb 8oz which was perfect for his more fluid stroke-play.

The Gloves

The hands are probably the most vulnerable area for a batsman; batsmen have to miss more games through injury to the fingers and hands than any other part of the body. The problem for the batsman is that the fingers get trapped between a ball delivered at express pace and the bat handle, and the only thing that gives is the fingers. I haven't gone unscathed myself. I had to retire hurt with a broken finger in the 5th Test in Antigua in 1990 after I got hit by Courtney Walsh. Quite apart from the damage such an injury can do both to your career and enjoyment for the game, it can also have severe consequences for your team. Retiring hurt is as good as losing a wicket, and if you're playing a two innings game, it's the same as losing two, so always make sure that your gloves are up to the job. Since I broke my finger I have always batted with extra protection on my index and third finger.

Other Protection

Pads, box, and thigh guard are essential. The roll of the pad should come over the knee, and the top flap should come about half way up the thigh, and should just touch the thigh guard. Other items of protection may be worn, depending on the circumstances. If you are going to face fast bowling, I would always recommend a helmet and a fore-arm guard. My own helmet has side flaps over the ears, but has no grille or visor, but I wouldn't advise anybody to copy it. I've managed to convince myself that my ability to pick up the line of the ball is impaired by a visor; whether this is true or not has long since ceased to be relevant. As a result I've already been hit on the jaw once, and I'm resigned to the fact that it will probably happen again. But you needn't settle for this state of affairs. Get used to batting with a visor, and keep safe.

Other protection that you might want to consider is the chest protector and the inside thigh guard. I don't bother with either of these myself; I don't like to feel restricted when I'm batting, and the prospect of being hit helps to keep me on my toes. There's nothing like a ping on the inside of the thigh to get the adrenalin going and make me even more determined not to get out to that bowler. However, there's nothing wimpish about using extra protection, and if it makes you feel more comfortable at the crease, then my advice would be to go ahead and wear it.

In General

Unless you know your game inside out and know exactly what you want, always make sure that you buy your equipment from a store that has a wide selection in order to give yourself the best chance of making the right choice. Don't be afraid to ask the assistant for help, but don't allow yourself to be talked into buying something with which you are not completely happy.

You may have often heard the commentators on TV criticize players for falling over because they have failed to wear spikes for batting. I can only endorse their criticisms. Always bat in spikes, or half and halves at least. Unfortunately, I am the least well-qualified person to give this advice, since I always bat in crepes.

Thankfully it's only got me into trouble on one occasion, but that was once too many. I was playing in a Sunday League game, slipped, and was embarrassingly run out. Fortunately my dismissal had no bearing on the final result as we won the match easily, but Peter Sainsbury, the Hampshire coach, gave me some stick anyway. Needless to say I haven't changed my ways, though. I was brought up on South African wickets where spikes were unnecessary, and I feel that I am too set in my ways to change now. Again, I'm afraid, it's very much a case of do as I say, not as I do.

Preparing to Bat

BATTING can be a very lonely occupation. There's your partner at the other end of the wicket, and your team mates in the pavilion, but when it is your turn to face it is essentially you against the opposition, all of whom are desperate for your downfall. Odds of 11 to 1 aren't good, and it's up to you to stack as many of the cards in your favour as possible. Preparing yourself, both physically and mentally, is vital. If you only think about what you have to do as you walk into bat, then it's probably too late.

Warming Up Exercises

Stretching and limbering up are an important part of any batsman's preparation. I always like to spend time loosening up my neck and shoulder muscles, rotating my lower spine, and stretching out my groin, hamstrings, and calves. These exercises should be done with smooth gentle movements; if you do them jerkily you will more than likely cause the very injuries you are trying to prevent.

These exercises perform two vital functions. By getting warmed up before you bat you are making sure that you will be able to respond to any situation from the moment you arrive at the crease. If your partner calls you for a quick single early in your innings, you want to be sure that you don't have to decline it either through sluggishness or fear of a pulled hamstring. You only have to see how many one-day games are decided by the odd run to realize how important taking every available single can be.

Stretching can also help to get the adrenalin going. Not only can this help your powers of concentration, but it can also help you to move quickly when you begin your innings. It is at the start of any innings that you are at your most vulnerable because you haven't got used to the light or the pace and bounce of the wicket. There's no point in adding to your problems by being heavy on your feet and slow to get into the right position. I am always amazed at how many people get out early on in their innings just because they have been slow to get into line.

Mental Preparation

Batting offers the player endless opportunities to come to terms with a problem, and to fail to do so. Perhaps more than any other game cricket is played in the mind. When you see a top-class performer have a run of low scores it is almost always because he has lost confidence, rather than because his technique has been exposed. So some form of mental preparation is necessary. Of course, one won't always get it right; everything one does is to some extent determined by one's moods, and sometimes no matter what one does, one just feels out of sorts. Part of the mental battle of batting is to accept that, and to be able to incorporate it into one's routine.

The easiest part of your preparation is to make sure you know exactly what is happening on the field of play. This may sound obvious, but it is surprising how many people walk out to bat without having any idea of whether the ball is moving off the seam or how many runs per over their team needs. This information should give you your basic motivation for the innings. You should know what shots are likely to

1

This is an exercise to stretch and loosen the shoulder muscles and rotate the lower spine.

2

Hold one end of the bat in either hand and push each shoulder back in turn to loosen the muscles.

be risky, and how much time you have to play yourself in before you go out to bat, and, when you do get to the crease, it should be with the intention that you will stay there until the match is won.

Never forget that the game can appear a great deal more difficult from the boundary's edge. The sight of a snarling fast bowler running in hard and making the opening batsmen duck and weave or play and miss, can send shivers of panic through a batting side. If this happens, don't bother to watch the game. The batsman may be just having a bad day, and making the fast bowler appear better than he is. Things may very well be different when you go into bat. Spend the time trying to feed your mind positive thoughts. This won't always work, but it will more often than not, because the mind has a tendency to believe the information it is fed.

One thing that may help in this is a process called visualization. It is something that worked well for Sir

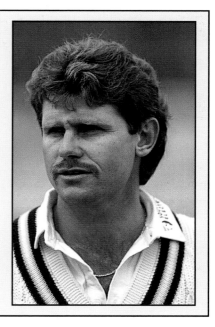

Robin's Tips

■ Stretch to get your body loose before batting. It will prevent injuries and help your performance.
■ Try to feed your mind positive thoughts by imagining yourself being successful. Don't worry if it doesn't work every time – you're only human after all.
■ Study the field placings. A few quick singles can do wonders for your confidence and irritate the opposition.

Richard Hadlee and my brother, Chris, and although I am no expert at it, it has paid dividends for me, too. Visualization is the art of imagining yourself being successful. Before an innings, I will see myself walking out to bat, taking guard, facing my first ball, and hitting it in the middle of the bat. I will then see myself playing a whole range of strokes against the opposition bowlers. When I actually face my first ball, I already feel comfortable at the crease, and my confidence is improved because as far as I am concerned I have already successfully negotiated a few overs.

Studying the Field

The last part of your preparation should take place as you take guard to face your first ball. Always study the field to see where you can take a few singles early in the innings. Nothing improves the confidence so much as some quick runs under the belt. Is the cover fielder too deep? Can you sneak a single from a defensive push on the offside? Mind you, you should exercise some caution in this if your partner is Ian Botham. In a Test against New Zealand Ian thought that Geoff Boycott was scoring too slowly for England's good. So when Ian went out to bat, he looked around for where there wasn't a single, hit the ball there, and ran Boycott out!

Keep your back leg and heel pushing on the ground and lean forward in order to stretch the calf muscles.

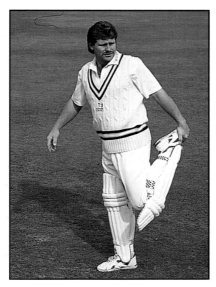

Stand up straight and pull each leg in turn up towards your bottom in order to stretch the quadriceps.

The Grip

YOUR bat is your friend. It should feel like an extension to your arms, and as familiar in your hands as a knife and fork. This may take time if you are a beginner, but it will happen provided that you adopt a comfortable grip. Very often this is the one that comes naturally. If you lay your bat face down in front of you with the handle pointing towards you, and bend down to pick it up as you would an axe, then you won't be far off the perfect grip. The only caveat is that a right-handed batsman should remember to pick up the bat with his left hand at the top of the handle, and a left-hander should do the opposite.

My own grip is not far from the classical grip. I place my left hand at the top of the handle in such a way that if I were to draw an imaginary line along the side of the bat and extend it up to my hand, it would cut through the knuckle of my index finger. I then place my right hand on the lower part of the handle so that the knuckle of my right thumb would be bisected by the same imaginary line running through my left index finger and the side of the bat.

Most people's grip will come within a few degrees of this, because there really isn't too much scope for variation. Someone with a truly orthodox grip might rotate the top hand a little in an anti-clockwise direction on the handle so that more of the back of the hand is facing the bowler, but, as I've said, it's being comfortable that counts. As long as your grip enables you to bring the bat down straight through the line of the ball, then you will probably be fine. Tom Graveney and Barry Richards used a grip which feels awkward to me. They both used to have the back of their top hand pointing towards the bowler in a grip that went well beyond the orthodox, but one would hesitate to say that two such great stroke-players were doing anything wrong.

The Distance between Your Hands

How far apart one holds one's hands is also a matter of preference. Imran Khan always liked to have a pronounced gap on the handle between his hands. He found that it helped him to control the bat better with his bottom hand, and that cutting and pulling against pace became much easier. I've never had that problem. In fact, I always use a double grip on the bottom of the handle so that I have less command over my bottom hand, and my top hand is made to grip the bat tightly. I

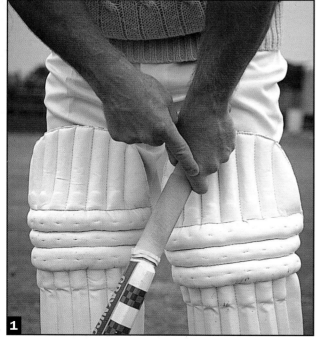

1 Hold the bat naturally so that the back of the hand faces the bowler.

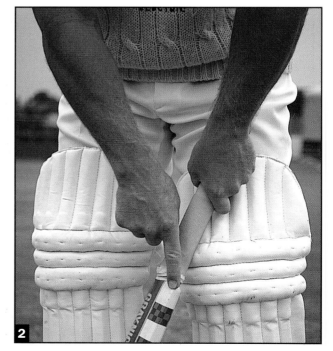

2 Note that the joint of my index finger makes a straight line with the edge of the bat.

believe that this gives me more control over my shots.

Maybe as a result of this, I like to have my hands close together on the bat. I don't have them so close together that they overlap, as they do in a golf grip, but having the little finger of my right hand in a position where it is just brushing against the thumb on my left hand feels right to me. Your hands should work as a team when batting; having them far apart on the handle is giving them far too much opportunity to work against one another.

High or Low on the Handle?

I also feel that the top hand should be positioned fairly near the top of the handle. You will certainly see some professionals who hold the bat so low on the handle that their bottom hand is practically on the blade. This I would not recommend;

Robin's Tips

■ Lay the bat face down in front of you with the handle pointing towards you. Pick it up as you would an axe, and your hands will be very nearly in the right position.
■ Keep your hands close together on the handle, so that they can work as a team in your stroke making.
■ Don't hold the bat too low on the handle; you won't get as much leverage in your shots, and it looks ugly.

quite apart from not being able to get so much leverage into your shots with such a low grip, it looks ugly. My grand-father used to say to me: 'If you can't be a cricketer, at least try to look like one.' It's advice that

I've always remembered, and is as apt for the grip as for any other part of the game. If you look like a cricketer when you hold the bat, the chances are that you will begin to play like one.

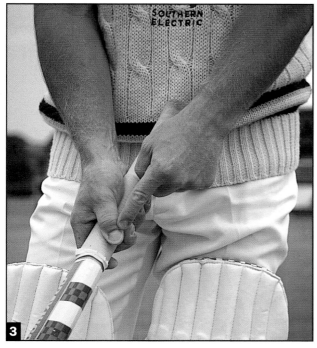

3

The knuckle of my right hand bisects the line between my left index finger and the edge of the bat.

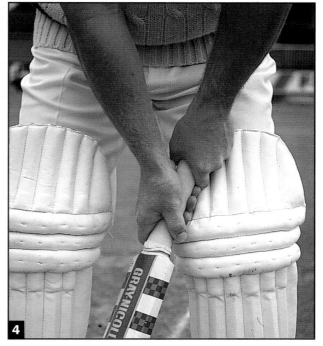

4

The final position: my hands are resting gently together, but not overlapping.

Taking Guard

YOUR first action on getting to the crease will be to take guard. The most common guard for a batsman is middle and leg, which as its name suggests, is positioned halfway between the middle and leg stumps, though some batsmen prefer to take either middle or leg stump. The purpose of taking guard is to let you know exactly where your head and feet are in relation to your stumps, and consequently whether the ball will hit the wicket or not.

As you become more experienced you may discover that you prefer a certain guard because it best suits your style of play. If you are particularly strong on the leg-side you may choose to bat on middle stump, as this will allow you to work more balls on the on-side if the bowler strays in line. Conversely, if you are a powerful off-side player you may want to bat on leg stump because this will give you more room to hit the ball through the covers.

If you are a beginner to the game I would recommend that you do as I do and bat on middle and leg. By taking this guard I find that my head settles nicely over the middle stump. You may have heard people talking about playing in the V when you first go out to bat. The V is the area between mid-on and mid-off, and is the safest place for a batsman to play the ball because he is playing with the full face of the bat. I feel that by having my head over middle stump, I am giving myself the best chance of playing in the V early in my innings.

Also, by taking middle and leg guard, with my head centred over the middle stump, I feel as if I generally know exactly where my off and leg stumps are. It might sound ridiculous that you can forget where your stumps are, but you would be amazed at the number of batsmen who do so and get out by playing at balls that they have no real need to hit.

Adjusting Your Guard

Sometimes you might want to experiment with a different guard to counteract the threat of a particular bowler. It doesn't always work though. Playing against Pakistan at Lord's in 1992 I had decided to bat on off stump against Mushtaq. I had had trouble at Edgbaston in picking the googly, and I thought that if I batted on off stump it wouldn't matter if I misread the wrong 'un; if I missed the ball it would hit me on the pad outside off-stump and I couldn't be given out lbw. Mushtaq saw that I was leaving my leg stump exposed, concentrated his attack on that side, and ended up bowling me round my legs.

Other efforts to disrupt a bowler can be more effective. The most usual place to take guard is with your back foot inside the crease, but some

The conventional position for the guard: my back foot is placed comfortably behind the batting crease, while my front foot is just outside.

In some circumstances you may have both feet outside the crease. Obviously this should not to be attempted when the wicket-keeper is standing up.

players like Graham Gooch often decide to take guard outside the crease against quick bowling, thus hoping to confuse the bowler's length and turn what would ordinarily be a good length ball into a half-volley. This isn't a tactic that I often use; in fact I tend to do exactly the opposite, and take guard right back on my stumps. I do this in one-day games against such bowlers as Dermot Reeve who are masters at the full length blockhole ball. By taking guard further back I am hoping to turn any yorker into a half-volley. This tactic is not without its dangers though, and you have to be careful not to tread on your stumps.

Limited Overs Guards

The most common time to change guard is in a one-day game when you need quick runs and can afford to take the odd risk. If a bowler is concentrating his attack on your legs, and has a heavily patrolled leg side field, it makes sense to step well

Robin's Tips

■ Choose the guard with which you feel most comfortable, and which allows you to play best through the V.
■ Take guard normally with your back foot inside the crease
■ Don't change your guard unnecessarily. It may end up upsetting you as much as it does the bowler.
■ If you do decide to change guard, do so decisively and positively.

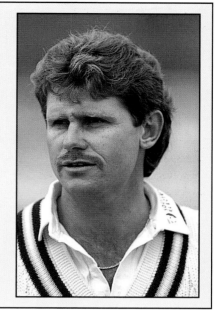

outside the leg stump, and try to hit the ball through the off-side. Derbyshire's Dominic Cork used this method to devastating effect in the 1993 Benson & Hedges Final. He used the width of the crease so intelligently that Wasim Akram had no answer, and Cork helped his county to an unlikely victory.

Such tactics should be used sparingly, and only then if you feel confident doing it. You stand just as much chance of upsetting yourself, as of upsetting the bowler. In general, I would suggest that you choose the guard that suits your style, and stick with it. It will be more than good enough for most situations.

The middle stump guard: Barry Richard's preferred guard is less common in first-class cricket today.

The middle and leg guard: the most common guard. it allows my head to focus directly over the middle stump.

The leg stump guard: this allows strong off-side players to play more of their shots through the off-side.

The Stance

THE key to a good stance is balance. No two deliveries are ever precisely the same, so a batsman can never predict the exact line, length, and pace of the next ball. To cope with this the batsman must have his legs comfortably apart, with the body weight evenly distributed on the balls of his feet, so that he is ready to go backwards or forwards depending on the demands of the delivery.

Cricket is a sideways-on game. All that the bowler should see of the right-handed batsman as he comes up to bowl is the left side of his body, with his head staring straight down the wicket. Some cricketers adopt a stance that completely contradicts these basic principles. Former England players Peter Willey and Kim Barnett stand almost square on at the crease, and have achieved great success by so doing. But it's not really a method that I would particularly endorse.

The classical stance is one where the batsman's feet are positioned either side of the crease, and parallel to it. The feet are neither so close together that the stance feels slightly unsteady, nor are they so far apart that the batsman cannot easily move into position for his shots. The toe of the bat rests behind the back foot, and the hands lean gently against the top of your front pad. The shoulders and upper body are relaxed, with the left elbow (for a right-hander) pointing straight down the wicket, and the head is held in such a way that the eyes are parallel to the ground.

The Smith Stance

What I have described above is the stance that I used until 1987. In that year I was playing in Australia, and unfortunately had to undergo surgery for haemorrhoids. The club for whom I was playing were keen that I should turn out for them four days after my operation, and I found that it was simply too painful to use my normal stance.

As a result, I had to open up my stance so that my legs were much further apart than usual. This change in stance altered my balance, and the most comfortable place to hold my bat was between my legs rather than behind the back one. I felt good at the wicket that day, and though I closed up my stance slightly as I recovered from the operation, it has remained essentially the same ever since.

In the end, though, you must choose a stance with which you personally feel relaxed, and which works for you. Don't feel as if you have to stick with the classical stance if you're not happy with it; but bear in mind that the greater your stance varies from the conventional, the more difficulties you may be making for yourself.

The Smith stance: my legs are further apart than in the classic stance and my bat rests between them.

The classic stance: my legs are slightly apart with the toe of my bat tucked behind the back foot.

The Pick-Up

THE only thing that matters with the pick-up, or back-lift, as it is otherwise known, is that it should be straight. Needless to say, there are a number of top-class batsmen who contradict this conventional wisdom by not picking their bats up straight, but theirs is not an example to follow. If the bat is picked-up straight, then the likelihood is that it will come down straight and give you the best chance of hitting the ball in the middle of the bat. You achieve this by controlling the pick-up with the top hand. If you push the bat back with the top hand it will go back straight; if you pull it with the bottom hand, the bat will be picked-up in the direction of second slip.

Some batsmen, like Graham Gooch, will pick the bat up high before the bowler has reached his delivery stride, while others will tap the crease with the bat, and make the back-lift part of the same movement as their stroke. The latter is the more usual, but either is sound. The reason why some batsmen prefer to pick-up the bat early is that they think that it gives them more time to play their shots against pace bowling. As with a lot of things in cricket, if this is what you believe then it is probably what will work best for you.

My stance precludes me from having a one movement back-lift. Because the bat is positioned between my feet, I would be bound to hit my back pad were I to draw it straight back. So my back-lift has become a two part movement. First I lift the bat and draw it back slightly, and then I complete the movement by pushing the bat back with my top hand.

Against pace bowling I will also incorporate a slight movement back

My bat is high and I'm perfectly still and balanced as I wait for the ball.

and across my stumps in the pick-up, in order to give me just that bit more time to play the ball. However, if you do this it is important not to keep your weight on the back foot. You must make sure that your weight is still evenly distributed on the balls of both feet as you get ready to play your shot.

Against fast bowling my first movement will be back and across the stumps, but my bat is still picked up straight.

In the pick-up keep your head still and allow your top hand to push the bat back.

The Forward Defensive

THE forward defensive may not be the most glamorous shot in the batsman's repertoire, but it is certainly one of the most important. The fact is that if you can't master the forward defensive, you probably won't survive long enough at the crease to dazzle the crowd with your more aggressive stroke-play. It is the basic shot that you will be looking to play early on to enable you to get the pace and feel of the wicket. It might be a little dull for spectators to watch the opening batsmen play forward and defensively at the start of the innings, but believe me, nothing gives the rest of the batting side more heart than to see the opposition bowlers becoming frustrated as ball after ball gets pushed back up the pitch.

Keeping Out the Good Length Delivery

The forward defensive is the batsman's response to the good length ball that is pitched either on the stumps or just outside the off stump. The good length ball is neither full enough to drive, nor short enough to play back to. As with all your shots, make sure that you commit yourself to the forward defensive as late as possible. You need to give yourself enough time to absorb all the information you require to play the shot safely. If you commit yourself too early, you may find, especially against the spinners, that the ball is of a different length to that which you had first imagined or that the bowler has extracted some late movement, either into or away from you, and that you are consequently playing down the wrong line.

Once you have picked the line and length of the ball, be decisive when you play, because it is equally as important not to be tentative in your defensive play as it is with your attacking shots. Don't take a half step towards the ball, but take a good, confident stride without going so far forward that you lose your balance. Don't let your hands get too low, and bring your bat down next to the pad. This is vital; many inexperienced, and some not so inexperienced, batsmen play what would otherwise be an immaculate forward defensive only to hear that

My head, knee and foot make a straight line, as I play the ball directly under my line of vision. I have taken a good positive stride forward to the pitch of the ball, not a shuffling half-step.

ominous death rattle of flying bails as the ball nips back between a gap that they have left between bat and pad and hits the stumps.

Head over the Ball

At the moment of impact you should be able to draw an imaginary line between your eyes, front knee, and foot, and your head should be directly over the ball. If you think of your eyes as a camera-computer you will realize that your brain will get the best picture of the ball if your eyes are directly above it. This will not only help to reduce your margin of error, it is also the source of good timing of the ball. People sometimes talk of timing as if it was some sort of mystery; it isn't. If you hit the ball directly under the gaze of your eyes, you will time it. How else can the ball sometimes race away to the boundary when the batsman has played no more than a defensive push?

Top Hand Control

The bat should also be kept straight and angled down. If you imagine that you have a hot potato under your front armpit, you will get your shoulders and elbow in the right position. If you drop your front shoulder, your bat will not come though straight and you will play across the line of the ball. It is the top hand that should control the stroke. If your bottom hand is in control, you may find that you have great difficulty in keeping the ball angled down and behind your front pad. This could well lead to your getting an edge or giving a return catch to the bowler.

The forward defensive does not vary with the type of bowling, and so, once you have mastered the

Robin's Tips

■ Wait as long as you can before committing to the shot, but when you've made up your mind play decisively.
■ Take a firm stride towards the pitch of the ball, and play your shot directly under the gaze of your eyes.
■ Keep your front shoulder and elbow held high. Remember the hot potato!
■ Your top hand is the one which the controls the shot.

principles, you have the basic means at your disposal to thwart any bowler. If you watch great front-foot players like Graeme Hick and Mike Gatting closely you will notice that they make exactly the same movements regardless of whether they are facing a quickie like Devon Malcolm or a spinner like Ian Salisbury. With Devon they might not need to come quite as far forward and they might play the ball a little higher, but the rest of the action will be identical.

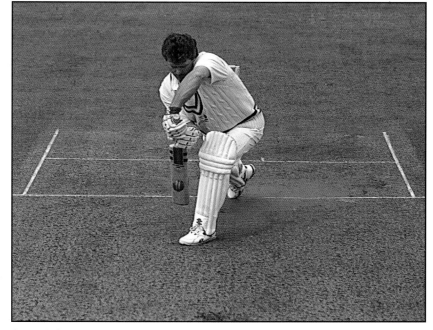

Stretch forward, keeping your left elbow high and your bat straight and angled down. Make sure there is no gap between your bat and pad.

The Backward Defensive

ON hard, bouncy wickets and against bowling attacks which are dominated by pace, the defensive shot that you will need the most is the backward defensive. If you have ever seen highlights of a Test series in the West Indies, you will know that a full-length delivery from Ambrose, Bishop, and Walsh is rarer than an apology from a government minister. But even if you are not going to be exposed to a battery of pace, the backward defensive is an essential part of the batsman's armoury.

This shot is played to a short ball that pitches on middle or off stump.

If the ball is going to miss off stump, and it's not wide enough to cut, then leave it alone. Unlike the forward defensive, which can pick up the odd run here and there, the backward defensive is purely a blocking shot. You won't be scoring any runs from it, so there's no point in playing a shot if the ball can't get you out. By playing defensively at a ball outside off stump, you are inviting an edge to the wicket-keeper or slips.

As with the forward defensive stroke, it is imperative that you should commit yourself to the shot as late as possible. This way you will

be able to tell exactly what the ball is doing. You can look fairly foolish leaving alone a ball pitched outside off stump only to find it moving back in off the seam, and either bowling you or trapping you lbw!

Later on in your innings you may find that you have the confidence to pull the very type of delivery to which you play the backward defensive early on. The difference between the two shots is that with the pull you are only giving yourself the width of the bat to make contact with the ball, while with the defensive shot you have the whole length. This makes the backward defensive a much safer shot and the much better bet early on before you have got attuned to the batting conditions.

Playing straight is the basis of a sound backward defensive. As the ball is bowled you move your back foot back and across your stumps to

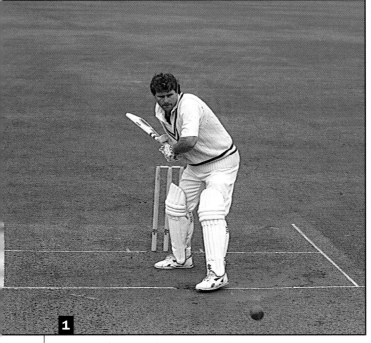

1

My back foot steps back and across the stumps to allow me to get into line.

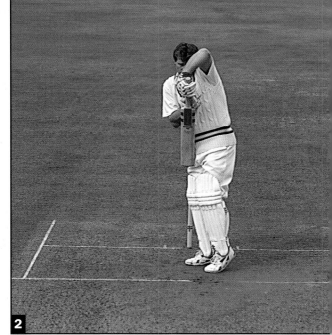

2

My bat is still perfectly straight and my body is right behind the ball as I prepare to play.

get you in line, and then bring your front foot back as well to help you keep your balance. Make sure that your back foot stays parallel to the crease, because this will help you to play straight. If your back foot points towards cover, your whole body twists round, and you end up chest on to the bowler. If this happens you won't be playing the ball directly under your eyes, your timing goes, and you become vulnerable to getting an edge or missing the ball entirely and being given out lbw.

Try to play the ball straight down into the ground. This is sometimes easier said than done when the ball rises more steeply than you thought. Here you can see another reason why it is so important to keep your weight on the balls of your feet. Even though you will have transferred most of the weight to your back foot as you shape to play the shot, if it is still in the balls of your feet you will be much quicker to make any adjustments, like going up on tip toes, to keep the ball under control.

Keeping your hands soft and relaxed, with the top hand in command of the stroke, will also help you to keep the ball down. As I've said before, this is purely a defensive shot and there is nothing to be gained by playing the ball firmly. Watch the ball all the way on to the middle of the bat, and let it just drop at your feet.

This shot is not technically demanding, but it can pose psychological difficulties for the batsman because it is often needed against fast bowling when there is the danger of physical injury. There is no real way round this, other than through practice. If you experience problems with this shot, it can be

The ball has bounced a little more than I expected and I've gone up on my toes to make sure I keep the ball down.

helpful to get a friend to lie on the ground and throw a ball up towards your chest. This will get you used to playing the shot, and as you become more confident you can get him to throw the ball a little harder, until you are ready to take on all-comers in the middle.

Robin's Tips

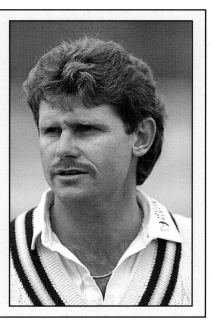

■ With this shot, if the ball is outside the off-stump, leave it. There's no point taking risks if the ball can't get you out.
■ Keep the weight on the balls of your feet so that you can make any late adjustments, and keep your back foot parallel to the crease. This will make it easier to stay sideways on and will ensure that you play straight.

The Off Drive

So much of the way the game is played has changed within the last thirty years, but if any shot could be said to symbolize the true timeless character of the game, it is the off-drive. Whether you are watching the likes of Don Bradman and Wally Hammond on a grainy black and white news-reel or David Gower and Graeme Hick in the flesh, you can't fail to be impressed by the sheer elegance and grace of this stroke.

Playing in the V

In the earlier section on the forward defensive I stressed the importance of playing in the V early in your innings. The off-drive is one of the main attacking shots that you should be looking to play when you first go in, precisely because you will be hitting the ball within the V. Whereas there are certain strokes that you shouldn't play before you have got your eye in, you should be prepared to use the off-drive from the word go. If you get the right ball in your first few deliveries, hit it; don't feel you have to pat it lamely back up the pitch. Nothing will give you greater confidence and irritates the bowler more than a crisply hit boundary from a new batsman.

The off-drive should be played to a half-volley or ball of fullish length, either on or just outside the off stump, and should be hit in the direction of mid-off, but should certainly go no squarer than extra cover. The basic mechanics of this shot are very similar to the forward defensive. You should take a good step towards the pitch of the ball, keeping your weight well on the front foot, with your front toe pointing towards mid-off to maintain balance. You should keep your top hand in command of the shot, lean

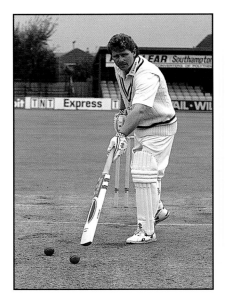

It is the ball I am pointing to closest to the stumps that is on the right line for the off drive.

into the ball, and strike it.

If the ball is of half-volley length you will hit it almost at the same time as it bounces, but if the ball is not quite so full in length, yet still full enough to drive, you must give yourself time to wait for the ball to

Playing the off-drive. I've carefully watched the ball all the way on to the bat, and my head and shoulders are pointing in the direction the ball is travelling.

My normal follow-through played during my 121 against India in Manchester: I like to punch at the ball, and my follow-through ends with my bat out in front of me.

come to you. Always play the ball directly under your line of sight. Don't go searching for the ball either by over-reaching in your step forward or by playing at the ball in front of your pads. If you do this, you will almost certainly mistime your shot, and you may well hit the ball at a catchable height into the outfield.

Different Follow-Throughs

Where the off-drive, and all other drives for that matter, differ from the forward defensive is in the follow-through. Whereas with the forward defensive you are allowed to stop over the ball, with the drive you continue the natural flow of the shot. The classical drive incorporates the full follow-through which ends with the bat behind one's head. However, contrary to many people's impressions, the follow-through is not a bottom hand, golf-swing-like, movement. Remember the hot potato from the forward defensive? Keep the front shoulder high, follow through with the top hand in control, and only when your arms are parallel to your shoulders should you break the hands and let the bat swing back behind your head.

Don't assume that the full follow-through is an essential part of the stroke. If you feel it helps you to play the shot well, then by all means use it; if not, then don't bother. David Gower was a great exponent of the full follow-through. He used to find that it helped him to get the rhythm of the shot, and even though he was a fairly slight man, very few people in world cricket could hit a drive more powerfully than him.

Personally speaking, I prefer to stop my follow-through with my arms out in front of me. This means

Robin's Tips

■ Get your weight forward and lean into the ball, but wait until it is directly under your line of sight before playing the shot.
■ Don't worry about the length of your follow-through. Do whatever helps you to play the shot best.
■ Look to play this shot early on in your innings if you get the opportunity. Don't feel you have to defend because you've only just gone in.

that I tend to punch at the ball, and probably have to hit the ball with a little more power to generate its speed over the outfield, but using this method I feel more in control of the shot. If your feet are not perfectly positioned when you play the shot, you can quite easily lose your balance when using the full

follow-through. Allan Lamb is another batsman who shortens the follow-through, but as I've already said there is no right or wrong in this.

My only advice if you are unsure about whether to stop your follow-through or not is to find out in the practice nets, rather than in the middle during a game.

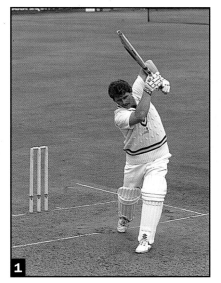

The full follow-through: instead of checking your follow-through, allow your hands to break ...

... and your bat to swing back behind your head.

The Cover Drive

A PERFECT example of how to play the cover drive was the stroke with which David Gower became, at the time, England's leading run scorer at Old Trafford in 1992. Aqib Javed bowled a wide half-volley, and David effortlessly leant into the ball to send it skimming to the boundary. It was a fitting way for him to break the record.

However, if you weren't lucky enough to be there or to see it on TV, don't panic. The cover drive is basically the same shot as the off-drive, but to a ball pitched between six inches and a foot outside the off stump. If the delivery is any wider it is generally best to leave it alone as you will be playing with your bat a long way from your body.

As the ball is wider than for the off-drive you must move your front foot further across to get to the pitch of it. One way to do this is to make sure your weight is leaning towards the ball, because then your foot will naturally come across. Again, as with the off-drive, throw your hands out after the ball to followthrough the shot, and use your chin, shoulder and elbow to pick your spot in the cover field. You may have wondered how certain cricketers always hit the gaps; the answer is simple – they aim. Whichever direction your chin, shoulders, and elbow are pointing in, that's where the ball will go.

I am pointing to the wider ball which is arriving on the right line for the cover drive.

Of course sometimes the ball goes squarer than you aimed for. At times this may be intentional, and at others not, but it will always happen when you play the ball late. If you are looking to hit the ball out square on the off side, rely on playing late, and never open the face of the bat to aim in that direction; if you do you will be playing with only half the face of the bat and stand a good chance of edging to gully.

A word of caution, though. The half-volley should always be a 4 ball, but it can also be a get out ball. Ian Botham took many of his 383 Test wickets with this delivery; some thought this was yet another sign of his outrageous luck, but there was far more to it than that. A full-length ball has much more time to swing and if you don't watch the ball carefully, you run the risk of being

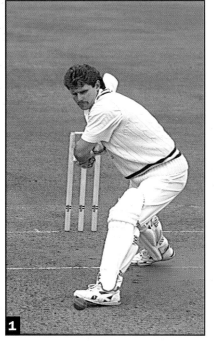

1 My front foot has come over in front of the stumps to make sure that I get to the pitch of the ball.

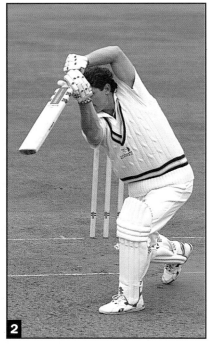

2 My left shoulder has been kept high to make sure that my top hand controls the shot.

bowled or lbw if the ball swings in and caught off the outside edge if it moves away. So concentrate hard.

Remain in control of the shot – in other words, do not believe that you have to try to knock the ball out of shape. It is more important to hit the ball smoothly, with your head still and a full swing of the bat.

Always rely on timing with the cover drive. Don't try to hit it too hard. Use your top hand to give you the direction, and let the right hand provide a bit of the power. Don't worry if your cover drive doesn't seem to have quite the elegance of David Gower's; after all, a 4 is a 4, even to us lesser mortals.

Concentrating hard on a half-volley served up by the New Zealand attack during the Headingley one-day game in May 1990. My chin, shoulders and elbow are all pointing in the same direction. That's the direction in which I want the ball to go and where the ball went – I think! If I had played the ball later, it would have gone squarer.

The On Drive

THIS is the most technically difficult shot in the whole of the batsman's repertoire. It is played to the half-volley or full length delivery that pitches on or outside the leg stump, and is hit in the direction of mid-on or mid-wicket.

Positioning the Feet

The main problem with this shot is that you are playing against the direction that your body naturally wants to go in. For the cover drive you merely have to lean your body into the shot and your feet will automatically land in the right place. For the on-drive you have to make your front foot get in the right position, which means that you will have to get much squarer on to the wicket than usual.

Here you can see how vital it is to keep your weight on the balls of your feet; if you play the shot correctly it's a certain four runs, but if you get it wrong you can easily get yourself out. If you fail to get your foot round, and your weight is still leaning over towards the off-side, then you will find yourself playing around your front pad, and probably lofting the ball towards mid-on or mid-wicket.

In your eagerness to get your body and front foot in position, don't forget that this shot is still controlled by the top hand. Remember the hot potato rule! If you allow your weight to be dragged round by your back shoulder, your bottom hand will begin to dominate the shot. When this happens your bat won't be coming through straight, and the blade of the bat will close. This will mean that not only are you less likely to hit the ball at all, but if you do, the ball may well go in the air and not in the direction you envisaged.

Making a Positive Movement

This is a shot with which you cannot be lazy. Ideally of course you won't be lazy with any strokes, but if you don't get everything quite right with most strokes you may well get away with it. With the on-drive you won't. So be especially positive when you play this shot. As ever, don't commit yourself to the shot until the last moment, and then move firmly towards the pitch of the ball. The wider the ball pitches down the leg side, the further your front foot must come across without letting yourself open up too much. Your front foot should still be pointing in the direction of mid-off.

This is a difficult shot, but it is playable, and few strokes give as much pleasure when they come off as a well timed on-drive.

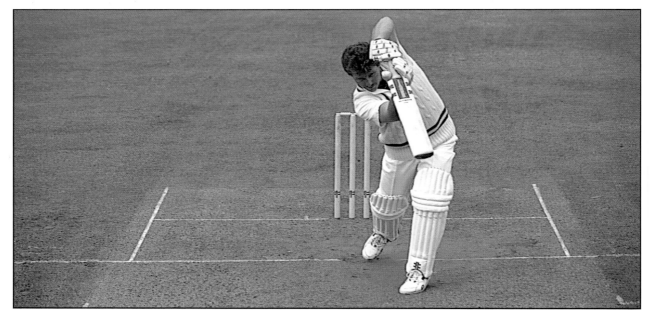

Even though I've opened up my stance to play the ball through mid-on, my front foot is still pointing in the direction of mid-off to make sure I keep my balance. Note that my left elbow and shoulder are kept high.

The Straight Drive

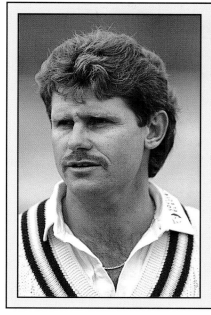

THE straight drive is almost identical to the off-drive. The only difference, as the name suggests, is that it is played to a ball that pitches in line with your middle stump. You simply plant your front foot firmly straight down the wicket and hit the ball back past the bowler between mid-off and mid-on.

All drives can be lofted, but the one that one sees most commonly is the straight drive. My advice to anyone who is thinking of lofting their shots is: 'Don't bother.' There is plenty of room along the ground to score all the runs you need. If you mistime a shot that is hit along the ground, the worst that can happen is

that you miss out on a boundary and fail to score. If you mistime a lofted shot you will be out.

If you must hit the ball in the air because the situation demands it or you just can't resist the temptation, then remember that the lofted shot is a technically correct shot. It is not a cross-batted shot, and you don't need to hit it too hard. It is the same shot

as the straight drive, but played to a ball that is a little shorter, more on the length of the forward defensive shot. Whatever you do, make sure you know where the fielders are!

It's a slightly risky, but very spectacular shot. Who can forget Ian Botham's first ball straight six off Craig McDermott in the Edgbaston Test of 1985?

Robin's Tips

■ It's almost always better to play the ball safely along the ground than to take up the challenge of clearing the fielders.

■ If you must hit the ball in the air, make sure that the ball you hit is a little shorter, and play an orthodox shot.

■ Take care backing-up when the ball is hit straight – if it brushes the bowler's hand and hits the stumps you're out!

Graeme Hick has everything right as he lofts a straight drive against Shane Warne at Old Trafford in 1993.

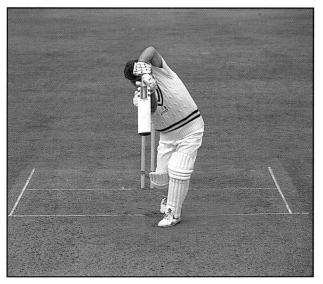

My front foot has gone straight down the wicket as I aim to play back past the bowler.

The Front Foot Leg Glance

THIS shot was particularly productive for me in the 1992 Test series against Pakistan. Throughout the summer the stock ball from Wasim and Waqar seemed to be the inswinging yorker. This delivery is deadly when it is bowled in the right place, but even bowlers as good as the two Pakistanis get it wrong from time to time. Sometimes the ball would swing more than they intended and sometimes their direction would be a little wayward, and I would be confronted with a full length delivery outside the leg stump. Such offerings are not to be ignored, and the front foot leg glance is ideal to exact full toll.

Breaking the Normal Rules

To play this shot you hit across your front pad. I know this sounds like a technical heresy, and it is the only stroke in the coaching manual for which it is recommended. The reason for this is that because the ball is generally pitching outside the leg stump and going wider still there is no danger. Even if you miss the ball completely and the ball raps you on the front pad you are in no danger of being given out lbw.

Your initial movement towards the ball will be the same as for the on-drive. You have to place your front foot down the wicket, but still keep your head over the ball. This is vital. At the risk of repeating myself, if your weight is falling over to the off-side and your eyes are no longer in line with the ball, then you will most likely either miss it or hit it in the air. This is quite hard to get right all the time, and you quite often see professional cricketers getting out in

this way. So always make sure you know where the fielders are, so that if by some mistake you do hit the ball in the air, you will stand a good chance of finding the gaps.

Where the shot varies from the on-drive is that as you bring the bat through you don't need to keep your front shoulder and elbow held high. Drop your front shoulder and allow the blade of the bat to close over the ball as you hit it. Some players prefer to keep their front pad firmly down the wicket when they play this shot. I'm not sure that this is actually the best way of doing it, because you are making life difficult for yourself. Admittedly in this case the worst that can happen is that you miss the ball, but then why pass up on certain runs?

What I prefer to do is to drag my front foot back slightly towards the leg side as I shape to play the shot. I find that I am then in no danger of getting my bat tangled up with my pad, and I can swing it through comfortably to make a clean contact with the ball. Also, with my front pad out of the way, I feel more balanced in the shot and can watch

1 My weight is on the front foot and my head is well over the ball as I shape to glance.

2 My bat is angled forward to keep the ball down as I close the face of the bat to play in front of my pad.

the ball all the way on to the bat. At the moment you hit the ball, break your wrists to guide the ball away.

Using the Pace of the Ball

This is a touch shot, and you don't need to put too much brute force into it. Few people have played this shot better than Viv Richards. Viv is an immensely powerful man, and often when he hit the ball, it stayed hit. Yet when he played the front foot leg glance, he appeared to just finesse the ball away. He was content to use the effort that the bowler had put into the ball to give the shot its pace, and he would merely be helping it on its way.

The cardinal sin with this shot is to try to be too skilful and hit the ball too fine. This stroke should be aimed between mid-wicket and backward square leg. You should never attempt to glance the ball down to the fine leg boundary. From time to time it may go there of its own accord when you hit the ball late by accident, but if you aim it there and are late on the shot then you are likely to give a catch to

Robin's Tips

■ After your initial forward movement, drag the front foot away to the leg side so that you have enough room to bring the bat through and make clean contact with the ball.
■ Never try to hit the ball too fine. Aim to play this shot between mid-wicket and backward square leg. This way, if you are late on the shot you will still be safe.
■ Don't try to overhit it. Use the speed of the ball.

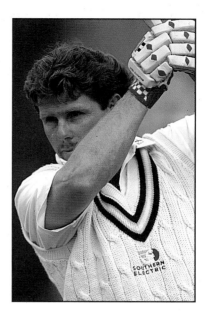

the wicket-keeper or leg slip.

I made this mistake myself during the 1989 Test series against the Australians. In the first innings of the 4th Test at Old Trafford I had scored my maiden Test hundred and I was feeling pretty pleased with myself. I was full of confidence when I went out to bat in the second innings and I tried to be too clever by half. Along came a full length delivery outside the leg stump from

Terry Alderman; my eyes lit up, and I thought: 'Runs.' I tried to guide the ball to fine leg instead of being content to play the ball square, played too late at the ball and got a much thinner contact than I had intended, and Ian Healy took a spectacular catch behind the wicket down the leg side. I might add that I wasn't quite so thrilled with my single run as I had been with my first innings effort!

My body weight begins to switch to the off-side as I start my follow-through.

My hands have broken on the bat, and I am square to the wicket as I complete my follow-through.

The Sweep

ANY shot that involves hitting across the line of the ball incurs an element of risk, and the sweep is no exception. It is played mainly against the spinners, and played correctly, can be a great accumulator of runs for you.

It is not an easy shot, and you should practise hard at it before using it in the middle. The ball you should play it at is the good length delivery outside the leg stump. You should be looking to play as near to the pitch of the ball as possible; sometimes, you may even over-reach and hit the ball on the full. In fact, it's far better to do this than not get far enough forward.

Stretch your front leg down the wicket in line with the ball and bend your knee; your back knee will automatically bend as well. Don't worry about how low your back knee gets; some batsmen play the shot with their back leg kneeling on the ground. Swing the bat out ahead of you by throwing your arms forward to meet the ball. When you hit the ball, the bat should be almost horizontal to the ground, with the blade slightly turned over to keep the ball on the ground.

The sweep is a perfectly safe shot to the off-spinner pitched outside leg stump. If the ball turns at all, it will do so even further away from the leg stump and there is no danger of being given out lbw. However, if you attempt the sweep against the leg-spinner or left-armer you have to be especially careful. Of course there is no danger of lbw, but there is of being bowled behind your legs.

The only way to counteract this is to make sure that your front pad is firmly behind the line of the ball, so that if you miss it, the pad can act as a second line of defence. Even if your pad is in the right place, sweeping against the spin is never to be wholeheartedly recommended. It is much too easy to get a top edge and knock up a simple catch.

English off-spinners tend to bowl very much wicket to wicket, which can make the sweep a risky option, because if you miss you will either be bowled or lbw. Nevertheless, batsmen do successfully sweep the off-spinners off the stumps. The key here is to keep your head as still as possible, so that you can watch the ball all the way on to the bat. This is important with any shot, but especially with the sweep as you are playing across the line and with the ball well ahead of your line of vision.

A further tip for sweeping on the stumps is to always make sure that you get your front foot well down the wicket. This helps you to play the shot properly and makes it more difficult for the umpire to give you out if you miss it. Some batsmen even sweep, or lap, a ball pitched on, or outside, off-stump. Here you are playing the ball entirely on length, rather than line, and it is a shot that is best avoided. Your team mates are not going to be too impressed if you play against the line to leg and your off stump is uprooted.

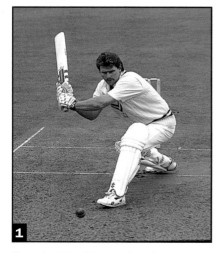

1 I've stretched forward as far as I comfortably can and my front pad is well in line with the ball.

2 My bat is almost horizontal as I make contact and the blade is angled to keep the ball down.

3 Concentrating hard on the ball. Even though I've already hit it my head is still focused on the point of contact.

The Paddle

A SLIGHT variation on the sweep is the paddle.

This is a more delicate shot than the sweep, and is played with very soft hands. You retain a much more upright stance, and play much later at the ball so that it runs down to fine leg. You should not use any power in this shot, but should let the pace of the ball do the work as you close the face of the bat over it. This isn't a shot that will bring you a hatful of runs, but it is a useful way of picking up a steady flow of singles.

Some Famous Exponents

Both Denis Compton and Alan Knott became renowned for their ability to sweep and paddle the ball. Denis Compton was a batting genius who made the sweep his trade-mark. Alan Knott used to say that the sweep was a pre-determined shot for him. He would make up his mind to play the shot before the ball had left the bowler's hand. If the ball wasn't of a length where he felt he could make the shot, he would improvise something. Someone with Alan's exceptional eye could get away with this, but few others could.

The Reverse Sweep

Certainly the reverse sweep is a predetermined shot, but that really is one only for the highly adventurous amongst us or the definitely suicidal. My advice is to keep it simple, and sweep only when you know the line and length of the ball.

I've used very little back-lift to paddle the ball round behind square.

There's no real follow-through as I just help the ball on its way.

Try not to hit the ball too hard and concentrate on getting the ball away square off the middle of the bat on the leg side. If you time and place the ball well you will pick up the odd boundary from time to time with this shot, but its prime function is to keep the scoreboard ticking over by picking up the odd ones and twos and to alternate the strike.

Breaking up the Bowler's Rhythm

If you have been pegged down by a spinner for some time and are needing to get things moving, then sweeping is a great way both to upset the bowler's rhythm by making him re-think his length and to get yourself to the safety of the non-striker's end.

Robin's Tips

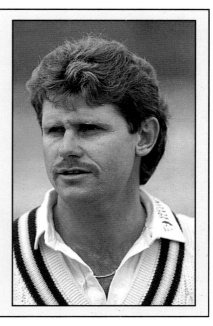

■ Be careful when trying to sweep or paddle the slow left-armer or leg-spinner. Keep your front pad right behind the line of the ball to avoid being bowled behind your legs.
■ When sweeping keep your head still and watch the ball right onto the bat.
■ Let the pace of the ball do all the work when playing the paddle and try not to hit the ball too hard if sweeping.

The Back Foot Drive

ALL attacking shots carry some element of risk, otherwise batsmen would never get out to them! Some players have based their entire career on the motto: 'I shall not get out', and as a consequence have deliberately cut out any shot with a hint of danger. They have set out to grind the bowlers down, content to keep their score ticking over with nudges and deflections and to leave the more aggressive stroke-play to their team mates. There is nothing wrong in this; every side needs a player who can stick around. All that matters is that you know whether you are a blocker or an attacker, and that you recognise the limitations of each approach.

David Gower was one of the finest backfoot drivers I have ever seen. The sight of him stepping back and caressing the fast bowlers through the covers was one to warm many a cold day at Southampton. Yet the backfoot drive was also David's weakness. Bowlers would often feed him that shot because they knew that although there was a chance that the ball would disappear through the off-side, there was also a fair possibility that he would play a loose stroke and the ball would end up in the hands of the wicket-keeper or slips.

The main point to bear in mind when playing this shot is to get into line and keep your weight over the ball. Whenever David got out to the backfoot drive it was because he had forgotten these cardinal rules. In the same way that the front foot drive is essentially a continuation of the forward defensive so the back foot drive is a continuation of the backward defensive.

As the ball is bowled your back foot should step back and across your stumps, but should remain parallel to the crease in order to keep you side on to the bowler. You will probably be hitting the ball quite high off the ground – somewhere between your knee and thigh – so make sure that you employ a decent back-lift. Your power and timing will again come from hitting the ball directly under your line of vision. Don't go searching for the ball so that you are playing with your bat a long way in front of your body. If you do, you won't hit the ball very hard, and it will most probably go in the air.

Your weight distribution is again vital. As you go back your weight will be largely on the back foot, yet as you play the ball your weight should be moving forward, pushing your body into the shot. Sometimes you may even finish the stroke with all your weight still on the back foot, because your front foot may be off the ground. This does not matter;

1 My back foot has gone back and across the stumps to get in line, and my eyes are still fixed firmly on the ball.

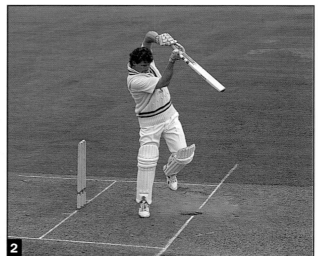

2 Even though my entire weight is on my back foot, I am still leaning into the shot.

what does is the direction your weight is travelling. If you lean back, pulling your head away from the ball, you will mistime it.

Your bat should come through straight, with your top hand in control, and your chin, shoulder, and elbow will again determine where on the off-side you will hit the ball. As with many other shots we have already discussed, never try to hit the ball too square, by closing the face of the bat. Sometimes the ball will go square when you are late on the shot, but you need to keep as big a margin of error for yourself as possible.

Selecting the Shot

The delivery to which you will shape to play the back foot drive is one which is pitched either on or just outside the off stump, and is shorter than a good length but not so short that you need to play defensively. The reason that you can attack the ball is that it will generally bounce at a nice height to enable you to play the shot comfortably. Occasionally the ball will bounce higher than you originally anticipated, and you can be in difficulties. If your weight is on the balls of your feet you may be able to get up on tiptoes and ride the ball, allowing you to keep control of the shot.

If you don't think that even by going up on tiptoes you will be able to keep you head over the ball, then pull out of the shot. Don't think that just because you have started to play a shot you are committed to going through with it. Just drop your hands to get your bat out the way, and let the ball go through harmlessly to the wicket-keeper.

Extra bounce and late movement off the seam can undo any backfoot drive, even if it is otherwise expertly

Playing a back foot drive against the West Indies in the 4th Test at Bridgetown in 1990 – an occasion when I used the full follow-through.

executed. Because the shot is played with a vertical bat, there is a greater possibility of getting an outside edge, so be careful. If you are playing on fast, bouncy wickets it may well be a good idea to consider omitting this shot from your repertoire, and restricting your off-side, back foot attacking shots to those played with a horizontal bat.

On a final note, be careful of over-confidence. Playing the back foot drive is often a sign that you are feeling confident, but don't allow

yourself to get carried away. On at least two occasions I've got myself out in Tests by trying to be too ambitious in my strokeplay. The first was against the West Indies at Trent Bridge, and the other against the Pakistanis at Headingley in 1992. Both times I played too carelessly at balls that I didn't need to hit. So keep an eye on how you are feeling whilst at the crease – at the very least it will save you the emotional energy of being furious with yourself when you've thrown your wicket away!

The Square Cut

1

I'm stepping back and across to get myself in line and to shift my weight on to the back foot.

BATSMEN often tend to be identified with one particular shot. For Ranjitsinjhi it was the leg glance; for Denis Compton it was the sweep; for Tom Graveney it was the cover drive; and for Geoff Boycott it was the forward defensive. For me it is the square cut. At times this irritates me because I think that people don't realize that I can play plenty of other shots as well, but nonetheless I suppose it is flattering to be thought to excel in one area at least.

It is no great surprise that the square cut should have become 'my shot' because I was brought up in South Africa where the wickets are often much faster and bouncier than they are in England. Wickets like these encourage bowlers to run in hard and pitch the ball short, making

batting a test of nerve as well as technique, and the square cut is the ideal attacking response in such circumstances. Anything loose on the off should go for four runs.

2

My back leg is slightly bent to give me better balance as I lean into the shot concentrating hard on the ball.

The Correct Distance from the Body

The square cut is played to the short rising ball that is wide outside the off stump. Never cut a ball that is too close to your body. Part of the success of the shot depends on how much leverage you can get. The moment you get tucked up, you can't time or control the shot and you may well get a top edge to the keeper. Occasionally the ball may pitch wide enough for the cut to be on, only for it to jag in towards you off the seam. There is nothing much you can do about this, except be on the look-out

for it. You will know if the bowler is capable of bringing the ball in, and if it happens, try to pull out of the shot, or make a little adjustment, and guide the ball down to third man.

Watching the Ball on to the Bat

Always watch the ball when playing this stroke. I know that this is something you should do for every delivery, but it is worth emphasizing here. It is amazing how easy it is for your eyes to leap out on stalks when you see the ball pitching invitingly halfway down the wicket and two

3

My wrists roll over as I play the shot to make sure the ball goes down towards the ground quickly.

feet outside the off stump. You think to yourself: 'This is a certain four', and you are so busy looking at where you are going to hit the ball that you forget to watch it on to the bat.

Your initial movement should be to get your rear leg back and across your stumps. Because the ball is wider than for other back foot off-side shots you should try to get a little further across than usual, but not so far that you lose your balance. Your knee should be a little bent, with your weight on the back foot, which, as ever, should be parallel to the crease, so that you are side on and ready to lean into the shot.

As you bring the bat down your front shoulder should begin to turn towards the ball, so that you hit over it, with the weight of your body in the shot. At the moment of contact the bat should be parallel to the ground and you roll the wrists so that, if you are a right-hander, your right hand goes over the left as you follow through. This last movement is to keep the ball on the ground. The very nature of the shot means that the ball must be in the air for some of its trajectory, but you should certainly be aiming for it to hit the ground 8–15 yards in front of

4

I break my wrists at the start of my follow-through still concentrating hard on the execution of the stroke.

you. Believe me, there's nothing worse than smashing a square cut off a ball that was just begging to be hit straight into the cover point's hands.

Robin's Tips

■ Don't play too close to your body. Lean into the shot and let your arms get a good leverage over the ball.
■ Roll your wrists over the ball at the moment of impact to keep the ball on the ground.
■ Don't get over-excited when you see what you think is a certain four runs, and don't try to hit the ball too hard. You will lean away from the shot and lose your timing.

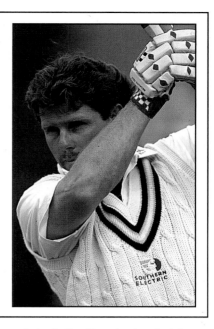

Power through Timing

One mistake that I often make when I play this shot is that I try to hit the ball too hard. There is no need for this. The power of your shot should come from the timing. If you try to force the shot you will start to lean away and lose control of the shot,

5

You can see that I'm still leaning into the shot as I complete a controlled follow-through.

and the ball will go in the air. The only thing that I can say in my defence is that the harder you hit the ball the more likely it is that if you do get an edge it will fly out of harm's reach well over the slips and gully's head. I also reckon that if I hit the ball hard enough, even if the ball goes straight to cover or point then these fielders have to be fairly alert and very brave to make the catch!

Cutting the Spinners

I've stressed that the cut is very much a shot to be used against quick short pitched bowling, but it is valuable against the spinners too. In the same way that you need to keep on your toes to counter any extra bounce from the pacemen, you should also make sure that you bend low enough to control the shot when cutting the spinners. A bottom edge can be equally as dangerous as a top edge; not only can you be caught behind but, especially when the ball is turning in to you, you can drag it on to your stumps.

The Late Cut

THIS, when executed well, is the most delicate and graceful shot of all, but it is rarely seen in first-class cricket, because the risks attached to playing it are so high. Wristy players with a wonderful eye, like Sunil Gavaskar and Alan Knott, could dare to late cut in a Test match, but for most of us it's a shot worth keeping for the one-day game when there aren't too many close fielders in attendance.

The late cut is your alternative option to the backfoot drive, in that they can both be played to the same delivery. The time you might choose to play it is when the off-side field is packed, making it difficult for you to find the gaps with the drive, whereas there is almost always a single to be had by trying to run the ball down towards third man.

Because the ball is rather fuller in length and closer to the stumps than it is for the square cut, it won't bounce so high and you won't be able to get any leverage or power into the shot. So the essential points to remember for the late cut are to bend low enough to get over the ball, and to let it just run off the face of your angled bat.

Correct Foot Placement

As with the square cut your rear leg should go back and across your stumps, but this time your foot should be pointing backwards in the direction of where you are planning to hit the ball, rather than remaining parallel to the crease. Your body will lean into the shot, and just as the ball is almost past you, you roll your wrists gently as you guide the ball to third man. Sir Don Bradman once suggested that when the shot is played perfectly the batsman will sometimes hit the ground with his bat after making contact with the ball, but this will depend entirely on how high it bounced in the first place.

Before the advent of the one-day game the late cut was used primarily against spinners, both because you have more time to play it but also because they rarely employ more than one slip. Nowadays it has also become a valid shot against the seamers late on in a limited overs game when there are no close fielders, and you are looking to keep the run rate up to target.

A final note of caution: never try to hit this shot too hard. A well-placed late cut may pick up the odd boundary for you, but remember that its primary purpose is to alternate the strike. If the ball either turns or swings into you then the shot becomes even more dangerous, so the important thing is not how hard you hit it, but whether you manage to hit it at all.

1

The ball hasn't bounced as high as for the square cut. I'm bending low to it and waiting until the ball is almost past me before playing my shot.

2

I've rolled my wrists to keep the ball down and let the ball just run off the face towards wide third man. Note that my back foot points in the direction of the shot.

The Upper Cut

IT'S hard to find a less orthodox shot than the upper cut, and as such it isn't one that I would coach any batsman at any level of cricket to play. If you do just about everything that I told you not to do when playing the square cut, then you will already have a fair idea of how to play the upper cut.

However, there have been some wonderful examples of batsmen playing this shot to great effect in recent years, so it is worth drawing it to your attention, if for no other reason than the academic. Alan Knott used to drive Denis Lillee and Jeff Thomson to distraction by repeatedly and deliberately flicking short-pitched balls over the heads of the slips and gullies. On another glorious occasion in Brisbane Ian Botham upper cut Merv Hughes for six over point on his way to his last Test hundred.

The upper cut is generally played to a ball that is shorter, and therefore bounces higher than for the square cut. There are two versions of the shot, which for the sake of convenience I shall call the Alan Knott and the Ian Botham. To play the Alan Knott, you lean back, and instead of rolling the wrists over the ball, you open the face of the bat to send the ball up and over the slips. There is no real need to hit the shot too hard, because the pace of the ball should do the work for you.

The Ian Botham is similar, except that it is hit squarer and with all the power you can summon. There should be no half measures with the upper cut; if you decide to go for it, then give it all you've got, because even if the ball doesn't go for six, it must carry the in-field.

Both versions are fraught with danger, and if you start to go for them too often the opposition will get wise to it. The sight of a fly-slip or a fielder three-quarters of the way to the cover boundary should be all you need to eliminate any thoughts of the upper cut from your mind.

1

I've had to pick my bat up much further than usual to cope with the extra bounce.

2

The face of the bat is open and angled underneath the ball to make sure I get it over the inner fielders.

3

The ball has bounced a little higher than I anticipated and I've had to go up on my toes to control the shot.

4

There are no half measures with this follow-through; I've leant back and given it everything.

The Pull

SOME batsmen, like Richie Richardson, have such a fine eye for the ball that they are prepared to pull from the moment they get to

1

I've picked up the line very early, and I'm nicely in position to select my spot in the leg-side field.

the crease. If the right length ball comes along, no matter where it pitches, they will smash it through the leg side. This, I might add, is not standard practice. The pull can be an immensely destructive shot because it can leave the bowler in two minds about what line to bowl, but it can also be dangerous. As far as I'm concerned, this is a potential get out shot, and as such is strictly for when you have got used to the wicket.

The pull is played to the same length delivery to which you would play the backward defensive early on in your innings. It is played entirely on length; whether it pitches on leg, middle, off or even outside the off

stump doesn't matter. Whatever the line, as the name of the shot indicates, the ball is pulled through the leg-side. The only difference that the line might make is to the direction in which you hit the ball. The further outside the off-side from which the ball is pulled, the more likely it is to go to mid-wicket, whereas if it is on middle and leg you will be looking to hit it squarer.

Getting Your Head in Line

Always make sure that your head is in line with the ball when you pull.

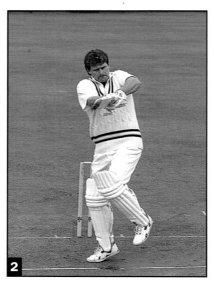

2

My weight is entirely on the back foot as I roll my wrists over the ball to keep it down.

So, the further on the off-side that the ball pitches, the further across you should get. Your weight should be on your back foot which should itself be parallel to the crease.

As you lean your body into the shot you should have your bat parallel to the ground while pivoting on your back leg so that you complete your follow-through with your head and body pointing in the direction of where you have hit the

ball. Don't worry about how far you pivot; Sir Don Bradman, who was the master of the pull shot, would sometimes end up with his front leg behind the stumps on the leg-side.

I would recommend that you play this shot along the ground, and you should again roll your wrists over the ball to ensure that this happens. If you happen to fancy your chances with the aerial route, then lean back as you hit the ball, and don't roll the wrists. It is rarely worthwhile taking this last option; as I've said before, if you mis-hit the ball in the air, you're out, if you mis-hit along the ground you've only missed out on a couple of runs. Whichever option you decide upon, make sure that you hit the ball hard. The pull is a no nonsense attacking shot, and there

3

I pivot on my back foot as the power of my follow-through pulls me towards the leg-side.

should be no holding back. Even if it goes to hand, if you've hit the ball hard there's a good chance that the fielder will drop it.

The pull is equally effective against all types of bowling. It is

Viv Richards was one of the finest pullers in the modern game; here he is handing out the treatment to his old adversary and friend, Ian Botham, during the fifth Test at the Oval in the 1984 'blackwash' series.

probably more commonly seen against the seamers, but it is more than useful against the spinners, as John Emburey so often demonstrates. I know that the

I have followed completely through and am looking intently in the direction of the ball to judge the run.

general rule when facing the slow bowlers is to play with the spin, but one can make an exception for the pull. If the ball is short enough to pull, then you will have enough time to hit the left-armers and the leg spinners through the on-side. If you are going to do this, then remember to get in position to pull as early as possible. Not only will you have more time to read the flight, you will also be able to place your shot more accurately.

I can't stress too greatly that length is all important when pulling. If you misread the ball and it is pitched further up than you imagine, then you are in desperate trouble. You won't have time to play the shot, and you will be bowled, lbw, or, at the very least, reduced to playing a short-arm jab in the direction of mid-wicket.

Also beware playing the pull even when you've been at the wicket for

some time, if you're not certain about the bounce of the wicket. Some wickets, especially in England, can be very two-paced. One ball may sit up nicely at waist height, while another delivery pitched on exactly the same length may get no higher than the knee roll of the pad. You must be very sure of yourself if you are going to pull on pitches like these.

However, I don't want to put you off playing this stroke. It's true that many of the best pullers, like Viv Richards, Gordon Greenidge, and Richie Richardson, were brought up on hard wickets, but it can be used effectively in English conditions. What makes this shot so useful is that it can make the opposition's field settings look ridiculous and can very quickly destroy the bowler's confidence. So by all means play the pull, but just be a little choosy about when you elect to do so.

The Hook

Robin's Tips

■ Always get inside the line of the ball, and help it on its way to fine leg.
■ Keep your eye on the ball. A short pitched ball can inflict nasty injuries if you lose sight of it or top-edge it into your face.
■ Don't be drawn into 'macho' games with the fast bowler.If you can see that the fielding captain has set a leg-side trap for you *don't* play the shot.

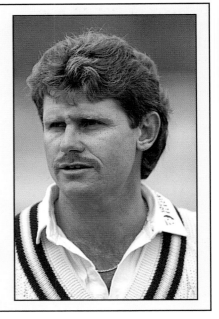

THERE'S nothing like the sight of a batsman hooking a fast bowler to get the spectators going. Who can forget the helmetless Ian Botham transforming what had been a desperate morning's play into a day that no one will ever forget, when he repeatedly hooked Denis Lillee for six from in front of his face whilst making a century at Old Trafford in 1981? Yet, without taking anything away from Ian, it has to be said that the gods were with him that day. Time and again he played the ball with his eyes closed and got top edges that went to safety.

If you need a reminder of how dangerous the hook can be, not just physically, but as a threat to your wicket, then think of the Australian opener, Andy Hilditch, whose Test career was ended in 1985 by being unable to resist it.

The hook is played to a ball that is even shorter than the one you would pull, and bounces to between head and shoulder height. Your initial movement will be back and across, so that you get inside the line of the ball. If you are a right-handed batsman you should be playing the ball just off your left ear. Because the ball bounces so high, it is extremely difficult to keep it down because you can't really roll your wrists over the ball, and so you should be aiming to do no more than just helping the ball on its way down to long leg.

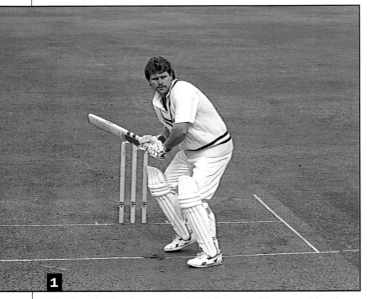

1

Playing the hook you must get into position quickly. I'm already going across the stumps as the bowler delivers.

2

I step inside the line, and I'm leaning away from the ball to give me room to play in front of my left shoulder.

To Hook or Not To Hook

All things considered, I believe that the risks involved in playing this shot aren't worth the potential benefits, and so I seldom play it. Not only are you in danger of being hit in the face, but you're unlikely to pick up many runs. You may get the ball away to the boundary once or twice, but as soon as the opposition captain sees that you're prepared to play the shot, he will position two men out deep behind square. Even if you play it well you'll only get a single, and if you top edge, you're out.

As most quickies tend to pitch short, you may worry that if you eliminate the hook from your repertoire you will be substantially reducing your scoring possibilities. I don't believe this is so. A head-high bouncer is a dangerous delivery, and as long as you show that you are willing to hook the bowler will keep on serving them up, because he knows that you will make a mistake sooner or later. If the bowler sees

that you are quite comfortable not playing a shot, he will soon realize that the bouncer is a waste of effort, and concentrate on another way of trying to get you out.

The hook is an exciting shot, but few matches are won by a batsman taking on a fast bowler in this way. Playing fast bowling is a war of

attrition for the most part. I reckon that I am lucky to get 10 run-scoring balls an hour against the West Indies, and while I will be looking to get full value from those deliveries, it is vital not to lose patience. Just remember that fast bowling is hard work, and that the quick bowlers will get tired long before you do.

4

I've rolled my wrists but there's no guarantee that the ball will go down.

My whole body has swung round in the follow-through – nevertheless, I'm still well balanced. Let's hope it went down and reached the boundary!

The Back Foot Leg Glance

CRICKET is a living game. All the different shots that I've discussed in the previous sections haven't been part of the game from time immemorial. They have evolved as the batsman's response to the problems that the bowlers have set him.

Origins of the Stroke

This is no better illustrated than with the leg glance. Prior to the late 1890s it had never previously been seen on an English cricket field, and it was only when an Indian prince called Kumar Shri Ranjitsinhji, who later played for England, invented the stroke that it began to become a recognizable and acceptable cricket shot.

People were shocked when Ranjitsinhji, playing for his adopted county, Sussex, first displayed his mastery of the leg glance. Neville Cardus, the celebrated cricket writer, recalled that: 'And then suddenly this visitation of dusky, supple legerdemain happened; a man was seen playing cricket as nobody in England could possibly have played it. The honest length ball was not met by the honest straight bat, but there was a flick of the wrist, and lo! the straight ball was charmed away to the leg boundary. And nobody quite saw or understood how it all happened.'

Professional batsmen today may not possess Ranji's artistry, but just about every single one will have a serviceable leg glance to call upon when required.

The Ball to Glance

The back foot leg glance is played to the similar length delivery to the backward defensive and the pull, and is a more than useful accumulator of runs in the early part of an innings. It is played to the ball that is angled in towards the hip, and you use the pace of the ball to run the ball behind square on the leg-side.

Latterday Exponents

Some players, like Ranjitsinhji at the turn of the century, and more recently Viv Richards and Javed Miandad, have such a fine eye for the ball that they can play the leg glance (back and front foot) to balls that are pitching on the line of middle stump. This is extremely dangerous, so don't try it; you are leaving your leg stump exposed, and even if you are not bowled you also run the risk of being trapped lbw if the ball doesn't bounce as high as you anticipate.

Getting Inside the Line

As with all back foot play, your first movement will be back and across. This will enable you to get inside the line of the ball. The main point to remember with this stroke is that you must give yourself enough room to bring the bat through freely. When a batsman gets into trouble with the leg glance it is more often than not because his front leg is impeding the shot. The result is that he either fails to make contact with the ball, or worse still, gets an inside edge on to the pad which sends the ball looping into the air to be caught by one of the fielders lurking close in on the leg-side.

Playing Front On

Because the ball is going down the leg-side and there is no danger of being given out lbw, this is a shot where you can safely get front on to

As with all shots played off the back foot my first movement is back and across the stumps.

the bowler. Unlike for the square cut where your back foot should be parallel to the crease, for the leg glance it should be pointing towards mid-off. As you bring your bat round to glance the ball, you should withdraw your front leg back towards the stumps, giving you room to play the shot.

As you make contact with the ball, drop your front shoulder, and close the face of the bat to let the ball run away on the leg-side. Again, don't try to hit the ball too fine. Aim just behind square to give yourself a small margin for error if you're late on the shot.

Retaining the Strike

The leg glance, both front and back foot, is a very useful shot to have in your batting armoury. It can be particularly valuable towards the end of an innings when you're looking to 'farm' the bowling in order to protect the weaker batsman by retaining the strike.

With the back foot glance, balls only just short of a length can be deflected with accurate placement past the leg-side field in order to pick

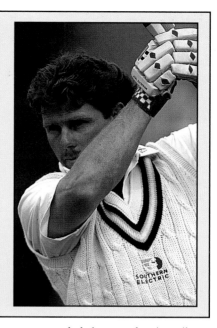

Robin's Tips

■ Open up your stance in order to get front on to the bowler, and get inside the line of the ball.
■ Make sure you get your front foot out of the way of your bat as you bring it in front of your body.
■ Don't try to hit the ball too fine. You will either miss it or get an edge on to your pad. Aim for just behind square to give you enough room for error.

up the single necessary to get to the other end.

Apart from its usefulness when looking for singles to retain the strike, it can also be very frustrating for a fast bowler who has bowled flat out at you to see you just casually flicking the ball around off your hip to the boundary. All that effort only to be deflected for four!

I know that in the earlier section on Choosing Your Equipment I

recommended that you bat in spikes, or half and halves, but the leg glance is one reason why I prefer to bat in crepes. I feel that I can get into position quicker because it's much easier to slide your front foot out of the way if there are no spikes holding you back. Even so, I wouldn't necessarily recommend that you based your batting footwear entirely on the benefits to be gained from one shot!

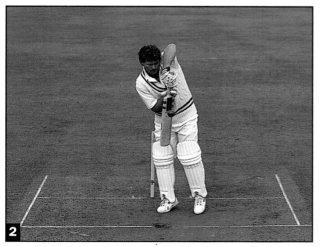

2 Both my feet are pointing towards mid-off as I've opened up my stance to allow me room to play.

3 I pull my front leg back to help me keep my balance in the follow-through.

Limited Overs Shots

innings, and besides which, the technique for a cover drive is the same whatever the game.

Taking Calculated Risks

However, there may come a time when you feel the need to take a few

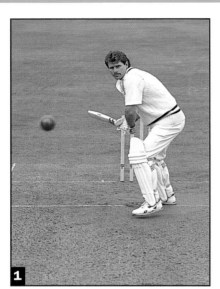

1

The ball will pitch well outside off stump which would ordinarily indicate an off-side shot.

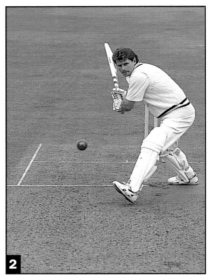

2

My front foot is advancing down the wicket as I prepare to play a cross-batted shot against the line.

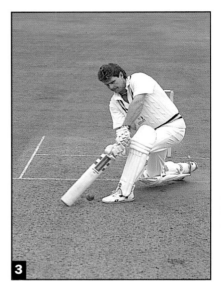

3

Even with an unorthodox shot, the basic rules of keeping your head still and your eyes on the ball still apply.

CONTROLLED aggression should be your watchword for one-day cricket. Unless you arrive at the wicket with something like 20 runs to get in two overs, in which case desperate measures really are called for, you are better off playing positive cricket using conventional stroke-play than having a slog.

Frustration is one of the batsman's greatest enemies in one-day cricket. Everyone has an off day when they don't seem to be able to time the ball, but the worst thing you can do is to lose concentration and try to hit your way out of trouble. It may work 10% of the time, but for the rest it won't, so the odds are that if you have a thrash your side will gain nothing and lose a wicket.

Whenever I'm struggling, I remind myself that the way to get out of trouble is to go back to basics. If I haven't got the timing to pick up boundaries, I can at least keep the scoreboard ticking over by looking for the ones and twos. So I will focus on where I can sneak a few singles. Picking up an extra run per over can make the difference between winning and losing a game.

There should be no real difference between a one-day game and a three-day game as far as your technique is concerned at the beginning of your innings. In both cases you should be looking to play straight. If you don't you're not going to survive long enough to try anything more exotic later in your

risks. It may be that the bowlers have settled into a comfortable rhythm, and are bowling so well to their fields that you just can't find the gaps anywhere, or it may be that the run rate has crept up to an unacceptable level.

Whatever your motive, make sure that the risks that you take are calculated risks, and that the shots that you play are as orthodox as possible. Always try to get as much in line with the ball as possible; you can then watch it all the way on to the middle of the bat.

Using the Crease

In the earlier section on Taking Guard I mentioned the importance of being able to use the crease in one-day cricket. If a bowler is concentrating his attack on your legs, and is bowling to a heavily guarded leg-side field, it obviously makes sense to try to force the ball through the off-side. To give yourself room to play this shot you back away to

4

My wrists have broken nicely and I am still well-balanced as I follow through fully with the shot.

leg with your back foot as the bowler reaches his delivery stride. Thereafter you should be looking to play a conventional stroke, so don't forget that your next movement should be to lean into the ball so that you hit it under your line of vision. Beware of moving too early; if the bowler spots what you are up to, he will bowl either on or outside the off stump and you will have trouble reaching the ball.

Playing against the Spin

In general, you should always try to play with the spin when facing the slow bowlers, but there are times when it is legitimate to go against this maxim. If a left-armer or leg-spinner is bowling just outside the off stump, turning the ball away from the bat in the hope that you will play out into the covers, then a good old-fashioned heave over mid-wicket is in order. Even if the ball is the googly and you miss you will have your front pad outside the line of the stumps, so you can't be out

lbw. Again, just because you are playing a cross-batted shot doesn't mean you should abandon the basics. Get your front foot as close to the pitch of the ball as you can, and follow through strongly, keeping your head down over the ball.

Unconventional Strokes

The reverse sweep has been used to great and sometimes not so great effect in one-day cricket by such luminaries as Ian Botham and Mike Gatting. I've never played this shot in my life, so I couldn't possibly tell you how to do it. If you want to find out, I suggest you ask Ian or Mike!

All these shots are basically ways to confuse and frustrate the bowler. They should never replace your normal strokes, and you can get by quite happily without them. After all, what you're trying to do is to score runs, and very often a conventional shot that is carefully placed and cleverly weighted will be far more effective than anything too adventurous.

1

I've both backed away to give my self more room to play and gone down the wicket to loft the ball over mid-off. I have reached the pitch of the ball for an orthodox shot.

2

It may not have been the normal ball to hit over mid-off, but there's nothing wrong with my final position. I have executed the shot according to the manuals.

Playing Fast Bowling

AT MOST levels of cricket it is the seam bowlers who predominate. The vast majority of sides take the field with three or four fast or medium-quick bowlers, and it is something of a rarity to find a team with more than one spinner. So it is readily apparent that you need a sound technique in playing pace to survive.

Getting into Line

Facing fast bowling is often a test of courage as much as of technique,

because the art is to get in line behind the ball. This is sometimes easier said than done when the ball is being propelled towards you at 90 mph. Personally, though, it's never been a problem for me, and I can say in all honesty that I relish the challenge of fast bowling. As a child, I was never physically afraid of anything, and nothing much has changed in adulthood. Indeed my most memorable piece of batting isn't a match-winning century, but the twenty minutes or so before tea in the second innings in Antigua in 1990. Out of the 14 deliveries I received, 13 were bouncers. I got hit on the body a few times, but it was totally exhilarating.

Protection

Nowadays in Test cricket, with helmets, plastic arm-guards, chest and thigh protectors available, the batsman has enough protection to

prevent the serious injuries, and you just have to take the view that any bumps and bruises you pick up in the course of an innings are just the price of the job. I know that this sounds a bit gung-ho, and I might well be saying something a little different and running away to square leg with the best of them once I've been hit a few more times, and my eyesight and reactions have deteriorated a little. But the truth is that cricket is not a game for wimps. If the bowler senses that you are scared he will go for your jugular, both metaphorically and literally.

Fast bowling is designed to intimidate. The bowler will be trying to wear you down with short-pitched deliveries that rear up towards your chest, throat, and head, and while you will certainly be using some of the back foot shots that we have already discussed, it is just as important to be able to get out of

Pulling Curtly Ambrose during my innings of 109 at The Oval in 1991. There are not many loose deliveries from a bowler of Curtly's standard and when they come your way you have to take advantage.

the way safely. Some balls are just too dangerous to make a shot worthwhile.

Evading the Bouncer

Ducking and swaying are not signs that you cannot cope with pace bowling, but signs that you can. The fast bowler wants to see you hopping about all over the place, and if every time he bowls a bouncer or a throat ball you just nonchalantly get out of the way, he will soon shift his line of attack. But ducking and swaying must be done properly. You only have to look at some injuries that have occurred on the cricket field to realize what happens otherwise. Nari Contractor and Ewan Chatfield were almost killed, and Andy Lloyd and Paul Terry had their Test careers ended before they had hardly started.

When to Duck

For the bouncer that gets up to head height or above, the best tactic for the batsman is to duck. To do this properly you must try to get inside the line of the ball, and then go all the way down. The most common mistakes are not keeping your eye on the ball, only half ducking, and leaving your bat waving in the air.

It is every bit as crucial to watch the ball when you're not playing a shot, as when you are. You need to be able to pick up the line and length to get safely out of the way, so never turn your back on the ball. Even if you've picked up the length of the ball correctly, sometimes the ball doesn't bounce as high as you anticipate, and if you haven't got properly out the way you will be hit. Equally there is no point getting your body underneath the ball if you then proceed to leave your bat in the air, where there is a chance it can be hit.

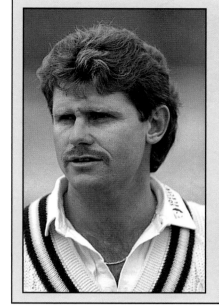

When to Sway

If the ball is pitched a little fuller it is generally best to sway out of the way. Try to get inside the line, because the real threat to the batsman is the ball that comes back in. If you have opted to lean back out of the way and the ball follows you, you will have to make some very late adjustments, and you can easily either be hit or end up on your backside!

The only time when it makes sense to sway back out of the way is if the ball is pitched so far over on the off-side that you are in no serious danger of being hit. However, once again, remember to drop your hands and keep your bat out of harm's way.

Dealing with Aggression

A large part of the contest between bowler and batsman takes place in the mind, and so I have worked out a number of mental routines that help me to cope. Fast bowling is an aggressive business, and many pace

Allan Lamb, a fine and courageous player of fast bowling for England.

bowlers get quite worked up and have a few choice words to say to you. Never reply and never let the bowler see you are rattled. He is trying to break your concentration, and if he manages to engage you in any sort of verbal interaction he knows that he's won, because your mind is at least partially concerned with something else.

One form of non-verbal exchange that is worth indulging in is staring at the bowler, because it's one that you cannot fail to win. Sometimes you will see a fast bowler stand and glower at a batsman who has played and missed or who has just hit him for four. Just glower back, because the fact is that the bowler will eventually have to turn round and walk back to his mark. This means that it is he who will have to break your gaze, and it is you who takes the psychological honours.

A fast bowler can take a long time to get through an over – time enough for you to psyche yourself out, if you're not careful.in your approach. So always try to relax

between deliveries; take a few deep breaths, and deliberately try to switch off. Try also to control your thoughts as the bowler runs in. I try to stretch the pitch in my mind. Instead of saying to myself: 'Twenty-two yards is terribly close, how am I possibly going to see the ball?', I push the far wicket back and say: 'Twenty-two yards is a long way away, I've got plenty of time.' It's a fairly obvious form of mental self-deception, but do try it because it works. If you think that you've got enough time to play, you will have.

Scoring off Fast Bowling

Because most fast bowlers will be aiming to pitch short, you will be looking to score most of your runs off the back foot, with your singles coming from nudges and deflections, and your boundaries from cuts and pulls. So remember the importance of moving in towards the ball after you have gone back and across your stumps to get in line.

Whenever I am up against pace, I try to think myself forward without

All wrong; I've no idea where the ball is and my bat's inviting trouble.

actually committing myself until the last possible moment. That way I am as mentally prepared as possible to

1 Even though I'm not going to play a shot, I've still got my eyes fixed firmly on the ball.

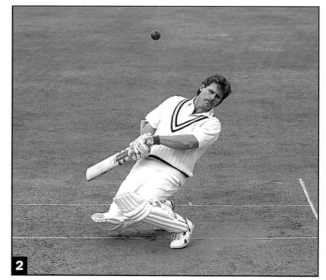

2 I've swayed out of the way, and I've also dropped my hands to keep my bat out of trouble.

get in the right place at the right time. Don't allow yourself to fall in the trap of anticipating the next delivery. Never forget that the bowler is perfectly entitled to pitch the ball in your half of the pitch. If you are on the lookout for a short ball every delivery, not only might you miss out on the occasional half-volley, but you might get out to the yorker, which can be a deadly delivery as Wasim Akram and Waqar Younis have proved, opening the bowling for Pakistan in recent seasons.

The bouncier the wicket, the more your aggressive shots should be played with a horizontal, rather than vertical, bat. On a pitch where the ball is rising steeply towards you, you have very little time to gauge the exact height of the ball accurately. As I mentioned when discussing the back foot drive, the straight bat offers a greater chance of catching an edge in such circumstances than a shot played with a horizontal bat.

Thinking about the Wicket

In many ways the hardest surface on which to play fast bowling is a pitch that is two-paced with uneven bounce. On a hard or soft wicket you will know roughly how high the ball will bounce, but on a two-paced wicket you may face one ball that is flying around your ears, and another that pitches on the same length and barely gets stump high. If you are playing on such a wicket, you generally have to put yourself in the hands of the Gods and play forward. You will certainly get hit more often by the balls that rise up, but you have to make saving your wicket your priority. If you go back to a ball that keeps low you are vulnerable to being bowled or trapped lbw.

Robin's Tips

■ Fast bowling is a test of nerve, so don't forget that mental techniques can be extremely useful in helping you to cope.
■ If you've played and missed forget about it and just concentrate on the next delivery.
■ Never reply to a fast bowler's verbal taunts and *never* let him see he's rattled you.

Of course, not every fast bowler relies on short-pitched bowling. Those that rely on seam and swing rather than sheer pace will pitch the ball much nearer the batsman to extract as much movement as possible. Against these bowlers you will be playing primarily off the front foot. So be prepared to play each ball strictly on its merits, and never dwell on a close shave. It's amazing how many batsmen get out to the very next ball after they have been beaten by the bowler.

Much better! I've ducked well under the ball, I've kept my bat down too, and there's not much for the bowler to get excited about.

Playing the Spinners

A S ANYONE who has watched me struggle in recent years against Pakistan, India, and Australia will know, I am not the world's greatest player of spin bowling. In many ways this should not come as too much of a surprise. I was brought up on hard, bouncy South African wickets where fast bowlers predominated, and I was never exposed to top quality spin bowling until comparatively recently.

Spinners like Mushtaq, Anil Kumble, and Shane Warne have heralded something of a revival for leg-spin in particular, and for spin in general. They have proved that the spinner needn't be the bowler who is used to contain the batting side when the fast bowlers haven't broken through or the specialist brought in

for wickets like Sydney which are renowned turners, but that he can be a genuine attacking match-winning bowler on many different kinds of surfaces. Where Mushtaq and Warne lead, so others will follow, and as a result of their example I am sure that many youngsters have been encouraged to take up spin bowling. All of which makes it more important than ever that a batsman, and I include myself here, should have a strong and secure technique against the slow bowlers.

Fast bowlers rely on sheer pace, with a bit of swing or movement off the seam thrown in, to take wickets. Spinners rely on deception. Every spinner has a stock delivery, be it the off or leg break, though Mushtaq seemed to bowl as many googlies as

leg breaks. While these may be wicket-taking balls, it is usually the variations of flight, length, and spin that will bring about the batsman's downfall.

A spinner will bowl a much fuller length than a medium pacer or quick bowler, because the batsman has all the time in the world to pick his spot in the field if he pitches short. He will be looking to draw you forward without giving you an opportunity to get to the pitch of the ball, and will be hoping that any turn and bounce that he can extract will defeat your forward shot.

Killing the Spin

When playing defensively to spin, the art is to get as far forward to the pitch of the ball as you can without over-balancing. Always try to smother the spin, because the further you are from the pitch of the ball the greater the opportunity for the ball to turn. Your bat should be firmly angled down beside your front pad, and should be held with soft hands. You should not be pushing at the

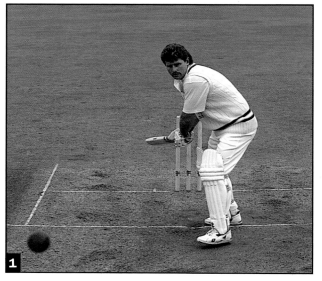

1

The ball is well pitched up and my first movement is to get my front foot forward.

2

I have my bat tucked closely behind my pad to give the umpire the impression that I am actually playing a shot.

The ball has pitched outside the line of off stump but by not playing a shot there is a possibility of lbw if it turned.

ball, but should be allowing the ball to hit the bat. The idea is that even if you do make an error in the shot and the ball catches an edge, you will have taken sufficient pace off the

ball to prevent it going to hand.

Beware of too loose a grip, though. In my second innings of the first Test at Old Trafford in 1993 I was so determined to play with soft

hands, having been caught at slip pushing at the ball in the first innings, that I played a sound defensive shot to the top spinner, only to watch in horror as the ball rolled off the bottom of my bat back onto the stumps.

Make sure that you watch the ball all the way on to the bat, and don't make too many assumptions about the type of ball the bowler has delivered before it has bounced. Just because the bowler may have appeared to have given the ball a lot of air, it doesn't mean that the ball is necessarily there to be hit. The spin that the bowler has imparted to the ball can make it pitch some one or two feet shorter than the flight would suggest, and if you are committed to the drive then you will either miss the ball entirely or be hopelessly early on the shot.

Even if the ball is short, you may

I am playing with an angled bat held gently in my hands so that if I do get an edge the ball won't travel as far as the slips.

not have as much time to play your shot as you first imagine. Both off and leg break bowlers generally have the top spinner in their repertoires. This delivery is a little short and gathers pace off the wicket once it has bounced. Many is the batsman who has been late on the shot and left stranded on the back foot to be bowled or lbw. So never relax for a moment, and play each ball as it comes; don't allow yourself to be lulled into a false sense of security.

The spinner will often be bowling with a couple of fielders close in on both sides, all of whom will be waiting for that faint edge on to pad. So remember that not playing a stroke is again a legitimate line of defence. If the ball cannot get you out, and you can't score from it, then there is nothing to gain, and everything to lose, by playing a shot. Remember the lbw laws though! If you are playing against a leg spinner who is pitching outside leg stump, as Shane Warne did for much of the Ashes series, then you can pad the ball away with impunity. Just make sure that you get your pad and body behind the ball so there is no risk of being bowled behind your pads.

You have to be altogether more careful about padding away when the ball is pitching outside the off stump. Obviously there is no danger if the ball is turning away from you, but if the ball is turning in and you are playing no shot, and in the opinion of the umpire the ball would have hit the stumps, then you can be given out lbw.

As a result many batsmen have perfected the technique of looking as though they are playing a shot when they are not. To do this you need to play as if you were playing forward, but keeping your bat tucked firmly behind the front pad so there is no danger of it making contact with the ball. Umpires will vary in their interpretation of whether you are playing a shot or not, so make sure you know the local customs, and get as far forward as possible to ensure you get any benefit of the doubt.

So how do you detect what sort of delivery the bowler is bowling? Judging by my own performances, perhaps I'm not the best authority on this, but I can tell you what the theory is and maybe you can also learn from my mistakes! Some batsmen can pick the delivery from the action of the bowler. Often there will be small tell-tale changes that indicate that he is bowling the googly or the top spinner. If you can pick the delivery this early, then you should have no problems. Some batsmen watch the rotation of the ball in the air to pick the delivery, and again this can give you those vital fractions of a second to select your shot and get in position.

If you can't do either of the above, then you can make a few general assumptions from the line of the ball and then play the ball from the crease. This is the least favourable option, because not only are you limited in your attacking play, but you also have less time to adjust for any turn or bounce. I had struggled against Mushtaq all summer long in 1992, because I couldn't pick him at all, but I eventually came up with a plan that worked in the second innings at The Oval.

I decided to play from the crease, and to treat every ball on off stump or outside as the googly, on the grounds that if it was the leg break

1 My back foot is behind the crease as the bowler delivers so that he doesn't have time to alter his length.

2 I take two steps down the wicket in order to get nearer the spot where the ball pitches.

then it would turn harmlessly past the outside edge. Various people had suggested I use this tactic earlier in the summer, but I had resisted because I couldn't see how I could score off Mushtaq if I didn't use my feet. As it happened I didn't score many, but I survived and helped myself to runs off the quicker bowlers. This wasn't the ideal counter to quality spin bowling, but it was effective, and it does show that even if your technique isn't the best you can flourish.

Using Your Feet

Spin bowlers love to get into a rhythm, and so the batsman should always be looking to upset them. The reason I was loath not to use my feet against Mushtaq was precisely because it enabled him to get into a good rhythm against me. I also think one of the reasons Shane Warne was so successful, not just against me, but against all the England batsmen, was because we were too defensive and allowed him to dominate. It's easy to say in retrospect, and the press and public would have had a field day if we had collapsed to a rash of

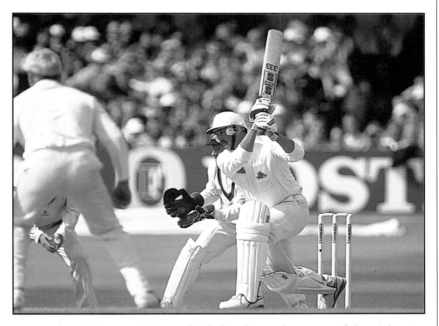

Graham Gooch is a good player of spin bowling and was one of the stalwarts of the English batting against the Australians in 1993.

attacking shots, but I think it's true.

Going down the wicket is the ideal way to disrupt the spinners' rhythm, because they are then unsure of what length to bowl. So much of cricket is a matter of confidence; a few steps down the wicket and a shot back past the bowler, and you can feel the confidence ebb from the bowler and flow into you. Whatever

you do, though, hit with the spin, unless the ball is extremely short.

There are no short cuts to playing spin well. It involves great concentration and good technique, both of which only come with practice. As I know only too well there is the world of difference between knowing what you are supposed to do, and doing it!

My front foot is now at the pitch of the ball, and I'm hitting the ball directly under my line of vision.

4

It doesn't matter that I've gone down the wicket. It's still an off-drive, and this is the perfect follow-through.

Running and Calling

When taking a quick single make sure that you run your bat in along the ground.

RUNS are the batsman's currency. There may be the odd innings where occupation of the crease is more important than scoring runs, but in general a batsman will be picked for his ability to score runs. At the end of any season each batsman will to some extent be judged on his average, which will be measured by the number of runs he has made divided by the number of innings he has played. So both on an individual and team basis it is vital that you make the most of any run scoring opportunities you have.

Running between the wickets should be a co-ordinated activity between two batsmen. So don't think that you can switch off and relax just because you are at the non-striker's end. You must be just as alert and assiduous in looking for runs for your partner as you are for yourself. When you are at the non-striker's end you should make sure that you back up properly. I'm not suggesting that you should try to steal a march on the bowler by taking off down the wicket before he has even bowled, because that is cheating, but you should be looking to back up by a couple of yards.

As a general rule of thumb, if the ball goes in front of the wicket then it is the batsman's call, and if it goes behind then it is the non-striker's. Calling should be restricted to 'Yes', 'No', and 'Wait'. Anything else just confuses the issue. 'Go' can sound remarkably like 'No' in the heat of the moment. When you call, or are called for, a run you should set off without hesitation. Most people are run out by a yard at most, which represents a fraction of a second's dithering.

You should always be on the look-out for singles. In any one-day game it is the amount of singles rather than boundaries that will generally decide who comes out on top. A well-taken single can irritate a bowling side greatly, and so is of immense psychological as well as

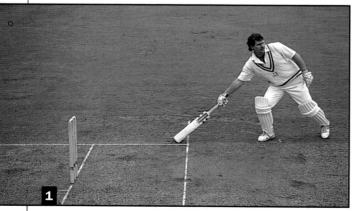

1

Make sure that you know the exact position of the ball and the fielders before you set off for another run.

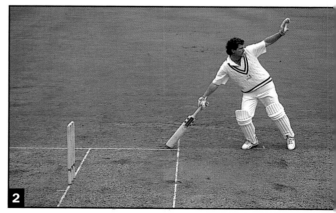

2

Communication is vital in running. If in any doubt about a run 'Wait' and back this up with a hand signal.

numerical value. To take quick singles you have to be alert to a variety of factors.

You must accurately judge how much weight is on the shot, and you must always know your fielders. You would certainly think twice if you looked up to find a Mark Ramprakash. Likewise it helps to know if a fielder is right- or left-handed, because a well-placed shot to the opposite hand almost always means a comfortable single.

Also make sure you know your ground. I was run out by Curtly Ambrose at Headingley in 1991 when I forgot that the ball gathers pace as it rolls down the hill at the Football Stand End. As a result it reached Curtly much quicker than I had anticipated, and I was run out by inches going for the second run.

Make sure you keep an eye on the ball as you turn for a second or third run. Never turn blind; always swap the bat from one hand to the other so that you never have to turn with your back to the ball. You should be looking to exert pressure on the fielders, and one way of doing this is always to run the first run quickly, because it can induce the

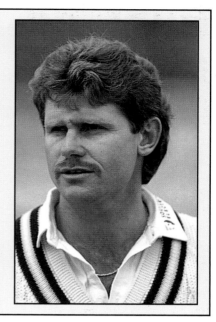

Robin's Tips

■ There are only three calls when running – Yes, No, and Wait.

■ Never turn for a second or third run while you have your back to the fielder. Swap your bat to the other hand if necessary so that you can always see what is going on in the field.

■ Always back up and put as much pressure on the fielding side as you can without endangering your wicket.

occasional fumble. Never assume you know exactly how many runs you will get with each shot. A batsman will sometimes stroll up the wicket, thinking the ball is on its way to the boundary, only to find that the fielder has pulled the ball up short, and that he has cheated himself out of a couple of runs.

Straying out of the Crease

However, do exercise some caution in your eagerness to score. A misfield does not automatically mean that you can take an extra run. Also against spin you should be especially careful about the placement of your feet. It's all very well trying to push along the run rate by giving the bowler the charge, but you will probably be stumped if you miss. Remember on the line is out; part of your back foot must break the front crease. There will always be days when you get the unplayable delivery, so don't add to your problems by getting yourself out needlessly.

Out – my foot may be behind the line but if it isn't grounded that's out.

In - my foot is just touching part of the ground behind the batting crease.

Principles of Batting

WHEN you first begin to learn the cricket skills I have covered in this book, batting is 80% technical and 20% psychological; by the time a player has reached first-class status those proportions are reversed. So it is to the mind one must turn for a greater understanding of the principles of batting.

Has batting ever seemed to you the most difficult task in the world one week, and effortless the next? The difference between the two is often not technique, but confidence. Confidence is a batsman's most treasured possession, because with it the game feels simple. No one knows precisely why people's levels of confidence can shift so dramatically, and a batsman's first duty is to recognize that there will be days when he feels out of sorts. If you don't, you will give up the game in frustration.

Yet that doesn't mean that you cannot try to stack the odds in your favour. Always try to fill your mind with positive thoughts. Even if you're feeling out of sorts at the crease, don't let on to the opposition.

A batsman needs to be arrogant enough to think that he can do the job. If your side needs to score 300 runs, you must believe that you are capable of getting the runs on your own; there should be no shirking of responsibility. If you even start to think that old so and so sitting in the pavilion with his pads on can get the runs if you get out, then you are already beaten.

Physically batsmen come in all shapes and sizes. Like his compatriot, Sunil Gavaskar, Sachin Tendulkar is hardly a giant but can dominate all types of bowling with an array of exciting, attacking shots.

Yet you also need to be humble enough to realize that you won't get the runs unless you obey the basic principles of the game. Never put pressure on your colleagues by throwing your wicket away through taking unnecessary risks. One of my first coaches, Grayson Heath, used to tell me to dedicate my first 50 runs to the week before when I probably hadn't scored as many as I should, the next 50 to this week, and the third 50 to the week after when I might be on the wrong end of an umpiring decision.

While you need the resilience and mental strength to cope with the demands of being in a 1 against 11 situation at the crease, you should never forget that you are also part of a team. There's no point in you making a slow, painstaking century when your side needs quick runs, nor in you making a spectacular 50 when what your side needs is crease occupation. The needs of the team should always take precedence over your own ambitions. Cricket is a team game played by individuals.

Once you've worked out what your team needs, then you must maintain your concentration to achieve it. If you need to score at six runs an over you must think sensibly about where you are going to get the runs. Look around the field and see where the gaps are, and what shots are on to which bowlers. Researching the opposition always helps, because you then know what each bowler can do. If you know that bowler A can't bowl the outswinger, and bowler B can't bowl the googly then you can eliminate those worries and plan your attack accordingly.

Every ball should be played on its merits, but you can have a fair idea of what the next delivery will be if you use your eyes and imagination. The position of the shiny side of the ball in the bowler's hand will generally tell you which way he is trying to swing it. If the bowler comes in close to the stumps expect an outswinger, while if he drops his front shoulder early, you know the ball will be short. If a spinner drops short, then he will give you a much fuller length delivery next ball to compensate. Try to put yourself in the bowler's mind; think about what he is trying to do, whether it be to get you out or stop you scoring, and plan accordingly.

The physical opposite of Tendulkar, Clive Lloyd was a big man and a superb striker of the ball who was also an excellent cover fielder in his early days.

Building an Innings

Each innings you play has to be carefully constructed. You don't play the same shots at the beginning that you would at the end.

Before you get to the crease you should have a good idea of what the team's needs are because that will define what sort of innings you are looking to play. If you need to score quickly there is no point in telling yourself that you have all the time in the world to play yourself in! Before every Test match I say to myself that I will be satisfied with 70–75 runs in the game. Obviously I would be disappointed if I ended my career with a Test average in the mid-thirties, but it is a respectable one for one match. So as I go out to bat I'm looking to chip away at that target.

It's quite normal to feel nervous to start with. The trick is to allow your nervousness to work for you rather than against you. The extra adrenalin can help you to move and think quicker. At the start of your innings you should be looking to score in the V between mid-off and mid-on, because you will then be playing with as straight a bat as possible. So cut out some of the more exotic strokes until after you have played yourself in.

Having said that, if the bowler gives you a juicy half-volley or long hop early on, don't pass up the opportunity to hit them. Just make sure that your head and feet are in the right place, and don't try to hit the ball too hard. But don't get frustrated or panicked if you are struggling to get off the mark. Be patient and look for the gaps for the quick single, and the runs will begin to flow.

The idea of scoring a century can seem ridiculous when you've been stuck on 0 for fifteen minutes. The idea is to break each innings up into manageable proportions, by setting yourself little challenges. Your first goal may be to get off the mark, your next to make 10. Find out what works for you.

The important thing is that as you reach each target, you should set yourself another and concentrate on that. The key to building a long innings is always to know what you are doing and why.

See yourself in by playing in the V to start with but remember – the team's need is paramount.

Graham Gooch has always been excellent at pacing an innings and is very rarely tied down for long. Here he attacks Warne in an attempt to break his stranglehold at Headingley in the 4th Test of 1993.

How to Practise

Net practice should always be taken seriously if you hope to derive some benefit. Bowlers should bowl from 22 yards and batsmen should treat each delivery on its merits.

THE whole purpose of practice is to make you feel in control and comfortable when you are at the wicket. You should always take it seriously, and as far as possible try to replicate the situations that you will encounter. So always wear the appropriate equipment. You will be fully kitted out when batting in the nets, but make sure that even if someone is giving you a few throw downs you are at least wearing a front pad. If you don't you will almost certainly not get your front leg in position for fear of being hit.

Everyone requires a different amount of practice, so just focus on what's right for you. A short practice approached positively and taken seriously may be better than a long half-hearted one. If you are going to spend your time in the nets trying to hit every ball for six, then you are probably wasting your time.

Try also to make sure that the bowlers who are bowling at you in the nets are taking the practice as seriously as you. It has never ceased to amaze me how many bowlers run in and overstep the crease by a yard in the nets. It's pointless as practice for them, and it's pointless for you. Not only will you have less time to pick up the flight of the ball, you will also be playing a trajectory you can never face in a real match situation.

It should go without saying that the purpose of practice is to help you improve, and so you should pay particular attention to those areas of your game that you don't find pleasant. If you're going to be facing a great deal of short-pitched bowling, then there's not much sense in practising your cover drives. Whenever I know that I'm going to be up against the quicks I make sure that the bowlers run in off the full 18 yards and bowl at my head. It's not always fun, but you've got to be masochistic about it.

A bowling machine is a great way of practising. Not only do you not need bowlers, but you can practise particular shots, and as your confidence increases you can turn up the speed with which the ball is delivered. Of course, you won't be able to have a net everywhere you play before you go out to bat. When you can't, make sure that you can at least have a few throw downs to feel the ball in the middle of the bat, and concentrate on getting yourself in the right frame of mind for the innings ahead.

Don't think of yourself as just a batsman. A lot more of your time will be spent fielding and you might as well be good at it and enjoy it. Being good requires plenty of practice.

Robin Smith's Best Squad

CHOOSING just twelve players is an invidious task. I can scarcely believe myself that I've been able to leave out such players as Greenidge, Gooch, Gower, Underwood, Procter, Garner, Dujon, Miandad, Bedi, Kapil Dev, and Abdul Qadir. Anyway, for better or worse, my squad selected from those players it has been my good fortune to play either with or against, is as follows.

Sunil Gavaskar and Barry Richards to open the batting. Sunil, 'the little master,' was equally assured against pace and spin, and was until recently the leading run scorer in Test cricket. He seemed to have endless patience, and could bat all day if required. Barry wasn't quite so renowned for his patience, but he was nonetheless a batting genius. He was so technically correct, and often seemed to have so much more time

Robin Smith's Best Squad

1	Sunil Gavaskar	8	Alan Knott
2	Barry Richards	9	Malcolm Marshall
3	Viv Richards (Capt.)	10	Dennis Lillee
4	Graeme Pollock	11	Michael Holding
5	Allan Border	12	Richard Hadlee
6	Ian Botham		
7	Imran Khan		

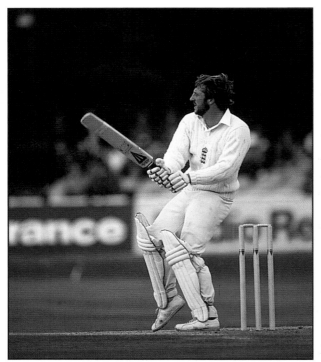

Ian Botham pictured during his famous innings of 149 not out against Australia at Headingley in 1981.

My old Hampshire team mate Malcolm Marshall, the greatest Test wicket-taker in West Indian cricket.

to play the ball than anyone else.

Viv Richards would go in first wicket down. He was immensely powerful, could conjure shots that other players couldn't even dream about, and on his day could destroy the best bowlers in the world. Viv has always been my absolute number 1 hero, and for that reason as much as his record for the West Indies, I would make him captain.

Two left-handers, Graeme Pollock and Allan Border, would follow at 4 and 5. Many people will never have seen Graeme play but I can assure you that he was one of the finest timers of the ball I have ever seen. If any of the top four failed you could rely on Allan Border to right the sinking ship. Time and again he came to Australia's rescue when his country was going through a bad patch in the mid-eigthties, and

now they are doing well again he is continuing to pile up the runs. Allan isn't always the most attractive player to watch, but he has an abundance of guts and will sell his wicket dearly.

Ian Botham and Imran Khan follow at 6 and 7. These two are not just two of the greatest all-rounders of their generation but of all time. Their records speak for themselves; they have both single-handedly won countless Test matches for their sides, with bat, ball, and personality.

My wicket-keeper and number 8 has to be Alan Knott. Quite simply he was the finest I've seen. He was so agile, and could take catches that other keepers couldn't get near. Knotty's batting is not to be under-estimated either.

The last three bowling places go to Malcolm Marshall, Denis Lillee, and Michael Holding. Malcolm

probably thinks he's in the side as an all-rounder, but useful though his runs have occasionally been, it is as a bowler that he makes the side. He isn't very tall for a fast bowler, but he's deceptively quick, with a whippy, skiddy action. Both Lillee and Holding qualify as the best fast bowlers I've played against. They had everything; pace, seam, and accuracy. Believe me, these two would be a real handful.

My twelfth player would be that great New Zealand all-rounder Sir Richard Hadlee. A superb bowler, he went on to become Test cricket's leading wicket taker and would certainly be in the side on a seaming wicket – probably in place of Imran who favoured swing.

So that's my team, and I'm confident that it could give any other a good run for their money.

The 'Master blaster', Viv Richards, captain of my team and my all time No. 1 batting hero.

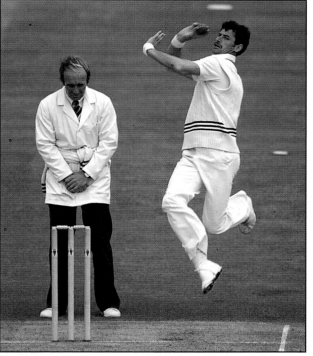

Sir Richard Hadlee, a superb bowler with one of the most technically correct and economical of actions.

Index